"I love everything about this book—the honest sights, the cross-generational conversation, and even the tension! Especially the tension. Because here's the thing: we can't fix what we refuse to face. This work helps us face the hard stuff about the church while honoring the good stuff, and it does so in a most winsome way that points to a future with hope."

Ruth Haley Barton, founder of the Transforming Center and author of *Life Together in Christ*

"Lots of people are walking away from church, and years of pain give them good reasons for doing so. But others are processing their pain in ways that help them imagine a better tomorrow for Christian congregations. That's what Nancy Beach and Samantha Beach Kiley do in *Next Sunday*. Each page rings with honesty, humility, and hard-won hope. The book feels like a generational passing of a baton, and that's something that older and younger readers will benefit from. Thanks to this mother-daughter writing team!"

Brian D. McLaren, author of *Faith After Doubt*

"In *Next Sunday*, Nancy and Samantha bring humanity and humility to strategic church leadership. It is refreshing to hear the voices of practitioners in the field of spiritual leadership who have the experiences to back up their content. I am grateful for this new and authentic work for those with a desire to create a new model of what leadership can look like in the church."

Nikki Lerner, culture coach and multicultural practitioner

"This is a memoir of two people, a mother and a daughter, who live in two different worlds and the same world at the same time. Reading this book is a jarring experience as each explores basic ideas, like community and Sunday morning church services, on their own from their own world. They're the same but not, at the same time. It disturbs me because I wonder if I can even know Samantha's world. I know Nancy's world, it's mostly mine. But they are siblings in Christ, and some inner-world reality transcends their two worlds. I needed this book."

Scot McKnight, professor of New Testament at Northern Seminary

"We are living in one of the most consequential times of the human story. Divides along economic, racial, cultural, and gender lines continue to widen. Conversations from pulpits to playgrounds, from halls of government to boardrooms and classrooms have been stymied to advance a way forward on these issues and a host of others. One entity that has not been consistent in these discussions is the church; she has yet to live out her full redemptive potential. Nancy and Samantha, as storytellers, speak with honesty, wisdom, and vulnerability as to what the church can—and indeed must—be in this pivotal moment. Hear their lament. Embrace the hope they offer in the transcendent."

Marcus "Goodie" Goodloe, Martin Luther King Jr. scholar and leadership development consultant

"I experience a mixture of resignation and heartbreak these days when I hear another story of someone I care about giving up on the church—resignation because it's so common, heartbreak because it shouldn't and needn't be so. *Next Sunday* is a much-needed book for our time. In these pages you'll find honesty, vulnerability, and a practical way forward. Nancy and Samantha lead us on a journey from resignation to renewal and from heartbreak to hope. There are still brighter days ahead for the church, and this book is a helpful guide down that path."

Jay Y. Kim, pastor and author of *Analog Church* and *Analog Christian*

"When Nancy Beach writes about church and worship, I want to read very carefully. When Nancy Beach and her daughter Samantha team up to write about church and worship, I have double the interest in seeing the important generational perspective by those who aren't just writing theoretically but have been in real ministry. This is a super-unique book that gives biblical, generational, and practical wisdom. I am getting copies for our Sunday team staff."

Dan Kimball, author of *How (Not) To Read the Bible*, on staff at Vintage Faith Church and Western Seminary

"In a season when many have walked away from the church, Nancy and Samantha have written a book for everyone who still wants to believe that church matters. *Next Sunday* is a profound gift for those wondering if the promises of the church are better than the problems of the church. It is for the person still searching for something real and redemptive within the ancient practice of ecclesia. It is for the person still holding on to hope that an imperfect church, led by imperfect leaders, filled with imperfect people, is still one of the world's most beautiful and transforming communities. Thank you, Nancy and Samantha, for giving us hope."

Jeanne Stevens, founding lead pastor of Soul City Church, Chicago, and author of *What's Here Now?*

"This book is timely, necessary reading. I couldn't put it down. Nancy Beach and Samantha Beach Kiley model through their shared writing how to ask hard questions and wrestle with the legacy of our faith communities; they show that doing so is an act of profound love and hospitality. I can't wait to buy a copy for so many people in my life whose faith compels them to acknowledge the messes that Christians have made, and who deeply want to address those wrongs together with their communities. This book offers the rare combination of loving criticism and pragmatic hope."

Jessica Goudeau, author of *After the Last Border: Two Families and the Story of Refuge in America*

"I don't know for how long, but I'm sure the church is in crisis. I'm a Hispanic pastor doing ministry in the States and even among 'my people' it's quite obvious that our main narrative is still fear, shame, and guilt. So every time I see somebody trying to understand this very moment in church history, I feel that we still have hope. If we don't understand our present, we don't have a future. Do you care about the church? You definitely need to read this book!"

César Soto, pastor of Amor Original in Austin, Texas

Nancy Beach and
Samantha Beach Kiley

Next Sunday

An Honest
Dialogue
About the
Future of
the Church

ivp

An imprint of InterVarsity Press
Downers Grove, Illinois

InterVarsity Press
P.O. Box 1400, Downers Grove, IL 60515-1426
ivpress.com
email@ivpress.com

InterVarsity Press® is a resource publishing division of InterVarsity Christian Fellowship/USA®. For information, visit intervarsity.org.

All Scripture quotations, unless otherwise indicated, are taken from The Holy Bible, New International Version®, NIV®. Copyright © 1973, 1978, 1984, 2011 by Biblica, Inc.™ Used by permission of Zondervan. All rights reserved worldwide. www.zondervan.com. The "NIV" and "New International Version" are trademarks registered in the United States Patent and Trademark Office by Biblica, Inc.™

While any stories in this book are true, some names and identifying information may have been changed to protect the privacy of individuals.

Published in association with The Bindery Agency, www.TheBinderyAgency.com.

The publisher cannot verify the accuracy or functionality of website URLs used in this book beyond the date of publication.

Cover design and image composite: David Fassett
Interior design: Daniel van Loon
Images: texture 2: sketchbook-paper-texture from True Grit Paper Supply
texture: TrueGrit, photocopy029

ISBN 978-1-5140-0302-2 (print)
ISBN 978-1-5140-0303-9 (digital)

Printed in the United States of America ∞

InterVarsity Press is committed to ecological stewardship and to the conservation of natural resources in all our operations. This book was printed using sustainably sourced paper.

Library of Congress Cataloging-in-Publication Data
A catalog record for this book is available from the Library of Congress.

P 25 24 23 22 21 20 19 18 17 16 15 14 13 12 11 10 9 8 7 6 5 4 3 2 1

Y 42 41 40 39 38 37 36 35 34 33 32 31 30 29 28 27 26 25 24 23 22

For our Lappidoths (Judges 4:4),

Warren and Will,

thank you for fanning our gifts into flames.

And for Baby Eloise—

and those who will come after—

and all that you will teach us.

Contents

Introduction

Debriefs are some of our favorite family memories. Hanging out in our kitchen, half of us sitting, half standing near the island, sipping Diet Coke while we devour a box of cookies—we love unpacking anything we just experienced together. It could be after Samantha's basketball game when we urged her to quit passing so much and just *shoot the ball*! Or laughing about Johanna's special soccer move she pulled out in almost all of her games. Our debriefs included evaluating every theater production the girls were a part of—our collection of programs and playbills is huge. Major moments were reviewed with tremendous detail, especially if something bombed, a line was forgotten, or a scene truly moved us.

All of our debriefs were highly specific, reviewing bad referee calls, missed lighting cues, and the awkward onstage kisses of teenage actors. We are a family who loves to talk, interrupting one another frequently, all in the name of judging . . . sorry, *evaluating*!

This debriefing energy was not confined to sports and theater—it also included church. Nancy's role as a pastor to artists created a bit of a curse. Our family struggles to fully experience anything without immediately reflecting on questions like, *How did that go? Was it clear, compelling, moving, or a waste of time? What would we do differently if we had a do-over? Do we think the message or artistic moment had its desired impact?* And although the dad in this scene is a left-brained business guy, he weighed in with strong opinions not only on sports but also on theater and church. All four of us were *all in* when it came to debriefs.

In recent years our conversations expanded to include Samantha's husband, Will. As someone who grew up mostly outside the church, he brings an entirely different perspective. The five of us engage in animated dialogue about the current and future state of the local church. We care deeply about churches thriving, both because of how most of our lives have been shaped and guided by various communities of faith and because we believe in the church as a force for restoration. We long for churches to flourish.

This book largely reflects those family conversations. We suspect that we are not alone and that many other families— from grandparents down to teenagers—share their assumptions, disappointments, suspicions, memories, apathy, and, yes, their hopes for the future of the church.

In fall 2019 Nancy was invited to speak to an annual gathering of Christian publishing executives in Boston. The assigned topic was daunting—forecasting the future of the church. The stakes for the future of the church could not be higher. In the "Great Opportunity" report, which was commissioned by Pinetops Foundation, we learned that half the people who grew up in church have already left. Churches, for the most part, are up against a culture increasingly filled with *Nones*—people with no religious affiliation. Nancy's thinking on the church's future was sparked by a message she heard from Pastor Ben Carcharias at a leadership conference. Building on those thoughts led to the seven distinctives described in this book. Together we asked, What will be most important for local churches going forward if they hope to thrive and not merely survive? Others will no doubt point out distinctives that are not on the list (prayer!), and we offer our perspective as humble learners who care deeply about the church and, like so many others, are just trying to figure it out. We do not come at these questions with an audacious sense of confidence or think we possess the answers or the magic ticket for churches to reach their full potential for the next generation.

This book includes two distinct voices—with a section from both of us on all seven subjects. Nancy brings her baby boomer perspective and experience on a team that built one of the most influential churches in the past forty years. Samantha is a millennial child of the megachurch and VeggieTales. She knows every word of the DC Talk *Jesus Freak* album and never missed an edition of *Brio* magazine. Her work as an artist—both in and outside the church—informs her perspective. And she has now gravitated toward a different kind of faith community from the one that first formed her.

Our church stories are also shaped by our identities as straight, White American women (who share 50 percent of our DNA!). While our gender brings certain expectations and limitations inside religious circles, we have the privilege of feeling comfortable in most pews. Our conversation focuses on our experiences in predominantly White churches in the United States and the patterns, challenges, and opportunities that lie before these congregations. Readers must not stop here. We believe tomorrow's church must center the stories of those who have struggled to feel welcome at our tables.

We write to open up the conversation, to share our journeys of discovery and our reflections on what is and what could be. Entire books have been written on each of these distinctives; we offer only a reflection on topics that surely warrant deeper study. We are not historians or academics but storytellers. Yet we believe there are some collective truths revealed in the particularities of what we and those we love have experienced.

This book is for every person who wants to believe that church still matters, even though so many of us have been disappointed, even wounded, along the way. Maybe, like us, some of your highest highs and lowest lows in life are connected to your church experience. As we wrote, we pictured our readers joining us around our kitchen, all of us still holding out hope that the church—all churches—can do better and choosing to be a constructive part of the solution rather than cave to cynical criticism. We believe in the unique potential of the local church to liberate and transform hearts, and repair and restore communities. So pull up a chair, grab a drink and a snack (if you were really in our kitchen, it'd be something full of sugar), and let's dig into the dialogue. And in the spirit of a true and fully engaged debrief, feel free to add your own comments in the margin!

Turn-and-Greet Terrors or Does Anyone Actually Care That I'm Here?

Creating Genuine Community

NANCY

The management team of Willow Creek Community Church met every Tuesday over lunch. I attended those meetings for the entire twenty-year run of my time on staff. We sat in a square of soft blue sectional couches up in our senior pastor's third-floor office, with a wall of windows overlooking the manmade lake on the church's sprawling hundred-acre property. Willow's food service, called Harvest, prepared a delicious meal for us every week. Balancing plates on our laps in front of a low coffee table, the ten of us would catch up one another on our weekends—stories of our children's antics and accomplishments, movies we saw on date nights, and sometimes how we were "really doing."

After our time of reconnecting, we would switch gears and dig into whatever agenda items faced us as we sought to lead the church. Some Tuesdays, other staff members were beckoned to join us to discuss ministry plans, vision, strategy stuff.

I vividly remember the day our executive pastor informed us that we would be hearing from a small group of the next generation, labeled Generation X by American culture. Our management team was composed of baby boomers, mostly in our forties. This group of earnest young people (in their twenties) wanted to design a new weekend experience and day-to-day ministry for their generation. I had an instant flashback to when I had been in their exact spot twenty years earlier, believing my parents' generation was clueless about how to do church effectively. I much preferred being on that other, younger side of the conversation!

They began by describing what they saw as the fundamental differences between the two generations. While they eagerly walked us through a well-prepared presentation, listing all the reasons why our approach to church wasn't working for them, I pasted a smile on my face, hoping to come across as open and curious while hiding my rising defensiveness. I think I faked it pretty well until I heard this statement: "Our generation highly values community. In fact, it's most important to us above the experience of Sunday morning." All I heard was what they did not say directly—*you boomers don't value community as much as we do.*

Maybe more than any other member of that management team, I was riled up by their assumption. Of course, I didn't lash out and say the words flying through my head at the moment: *Community is what this church was built on! How dare you try to hijack this value and claim it belongs to your generation exclusively! Everything I have built in the arts ministry of this church centered on a foundation of deep, authentic community. My team has been together the longest, and we are like family to one another!*

To this day my most treasured memories of ministry are not massive events—like when we crammed twenty thousand people into Chicago's United Center for the church's twentieth-anniversary celebration—or the original musicals we created for outreach, or the powerful Christmas and Holy Week services filled with moments of transcendence and wonder and beauty and God's holy presence. Those were all meaningful to me, but they cannot compare to the life-giving experiences of our little team.

My most precious ministry memories include the retreats our arts staff would take in a small Wisconsin cottage, sometimes laughing so hard over meals that tears ran down our cheeks, dancing around a tiny kitchen as we washed dishes to the sounds of Sister Sledge—"We are family. Get up everybody and sing." We honored one another as we reviewed video highlights from our services and presented homemade awards in our own version of the Oscars. That same team formed a circle on a deck of the cottage, and with a bowl of water and a few towels, we washed one another's feet as we confessed our sins of pride and envy, visibly serving our brothers and sisters.

We knew one another's stories. We worked through inevitable conflicts with one another and learned to say "I'm sorry." It wasn't all abundant joy. One day after an extremely difficult meeting when my team risked telling some hard truths to me, I walked to my car and slammed the door, thinking, *Community, shamunity! Who needs it?* (Such a mature, Christ-centered response!) But deep down, I knew *I* needed it.

I danced with raucous celebration at the weddings of Steve's daughters. I stood at the graveside of Pam's father as the bagpipes played terribly out of key on a dreadfully humid summer afternoon. My teammates showed up at the hospital when my toddler came down with a mysterious high fever. We didn't just do ministry together; we had the profound gift of doing life together. This included the major highs and lows of life along with the more ordinary, everyday moments we couldn't wait to share with one another. At Willow we would often say that doing ministry with people you love—*community*—is the hidden treasure that emerges in the midst of the cause. Ministry can be extremely hard in so many ways, and no one is in it for the pay. The remarkable and unexpected gift is all about the relationships we form as we do the work of the kingdom and catch one another's eyes, thinking, *I can't believe we get to do this together*.

I can hear some protests that of course a group of creative artists, "touchy-feely types," would value community. But what about more task-oriented, activist teams or those who are true introverts? My husband, Warren, is a factual kind of guy, a commodities trader who thinks in terms of numbers and ideas, not feelings, and who is most definitely an introvert. Warren has led various ministry initiatives as a volunteer. Early in our married life he took on the leadership role of a ministry called

"Good Sense." This was a thoughtful, intelligent group of volunteers who helped congregants understand what the Bible teaches about money and how we can honor God with our finances. Warren assembled a team of mostly left-brained accountant types to help lead and coach people to practice getting out of debt, establish a budget, save wisely, and give generously. Once a month this group of eight or ten volunteers would meet in our living room. Warren always had a flip chart ready to launch into his extremely full and very important agenda. I usually hung out in another part of the house. Before one of the meetings I asked Warren if he would like me to make a dessert for his team so they could linger and enjoy some time after the meeting. He said, "Why would I want to do that?"

I responded that maybe, just maybe, the people might want to talk a little about their personal lives, go beyond the agenda, get to know one another a bit. Warren was entirely unconvinced this was necessary but said okay to the brownies. The group started hanging out after the meeting was officially over. Stories were shared about the challenges of raising teenagers, caring for an elderly parent, unrealistic expectations at work, or the excitement of an upcoming vacation. And despite Warren's assumption that this group in particular wouldn't want to "do community," a community started to form anyway.

———

Our focus on the value of community in the local church must be informed by the bigger picture of the entire social fabric of American culture. Robert Putnam is a renowned social scientist and author who has done extensive research analyzing cultural trends over the past 140 years. In his fascinating book *The Upswing*, Putnam explains how America was once a highly individualistic society during the Gilded Age of the late 1800s. But with the dawn of the twentieth century this country gradually became more cooperative, peaking in the decade of the 1960s with high numbers of citizens engaging in all kinds of community groups, becoming increasingly a nation of joiners. Putnam says we moved from being an *I* society of rugged individualism to more of a *We* culture, and this trend included weekly attendance and volunteerism in a local church or synagogue.

Yet since the 1960s the trend has dramatically reversed. Putnam writes, "In greater numbers than ever before, Americans seem to have stopped believing that we are all in this together." Participation in almost every communal activity from unions to the PTA to Rotary Clubs is down. This cultural trend has had a huge impact on local churches. Baby boomers have memories of the *We* society but have also contributed to the decline back toward the *I* culture.

The truth is that every human was created to live in community with a few others. We used to say at Willow that everyone has a deep desire to know and be known, to love and be loved, to serve and be served. We see that Jesus himself invested in a community of friends and disciples, including Mary, Martha, and Lazarus— siblings who invited their Teacher into their home, where Jesus no doubt found rest, refuge, and joy.

But while our magnificent Creator has designed us to pursue connection with one another and modeled that for us, we must choose to move away from our tendency to isolate. All of this has been magnified by the hunkering down we experienced throughout the Covid-19 pandemic. Our movements back into connection have been tentative and wobbly and even frightening for some.

It's all too easy for us to minimize the significance of what it means to belong and to be known. I am concerned for anyone who shows up to do any kind of task at a church in the name of Jesus— whether it's sorting boxes at the food pantry, mowing a lawn, rehearsing worship music, or preparing a room for the children. Each volunteer has a life outside of the local church. Imagine the volunteer bass player in a worship band who shows up faithfully on a Wednesday night to rehearse. For two hours the group works through the songs to be used the following weekend. Maybe there's a short prayer at the start of rehearsal, but after that it's all about getting the music right. When the work is done, the team says their goodbyes, and the bass player walks out to his car in the parking lot.

What if earlier that day he had a tough conversation with his boss at work, or what if his daughter is struggling with a bully at school, or what if he got good news about a new job for his wife? I think he might feel a little empty and disappointed that no one in the worship band knew his story that day. He would not have felt known and seen. He might even be tempted to feel a little used, only wanted for his musical gift.

I realize it's not possible for every team that comes together for a task to also include an hour or more of sharing our lives with one another. Unless a small group is formed expressly for that purpose alone, it's just not realistic for most of us to carve out that time. However, I think there's a middle ground, a step that does not require major amounts of time but opens the door to volunteers feeling known and seen.

———

Allow me to move from theory to the extremely practical, with a couple of options for intentionally connecting with a team beyond the task. The first option works well at the start of the meeting or task. What if the group forms a circle—assuming it is less than ten people (if there are more than that, make more circles)—and going around the circle, each person is asked to answer a simple question: Since we were last together, what was a high point in your life? And what was a low point? To avoid stories getting too long and detailed, tell them they each have a total of a minute (or two if you're feeling generous) to share their high and low. As a leader you have introduced a sense of connection before the work begins. People can choose to follow up on what they hear at a later time, but every individual has a chance to speak a part of their story. And as a group we can rejoice with those who rejoice and mourn with those who mourn.

The second option works well at the close of the meeting or task time. Circle up, standing so that everyone knows this won't be long. Ask each person for one way we can specifically pray for them this next week. Tell them to say it in a sentence or two. Also encourage everyone to pay close attention to what the person on their left says because in a moment they will offer a short prayer for that person. In this way, during the brief prayer time, each person gets prayed for and each person prays for someone else. As you dismiss the group, individuals can choose whether to follow up with anyone. But my imaginary bass player would go to his car feeling a little more known and seen. In this way we break down the compartmentalization between our personal lives and our ministry service. And a sense of community starts to be built.

I believe that what has drawn many people to the local church in the past, and what will become *even more* essential going forward, is the desire to be a part of a genuine community. There is a mighty power in the telling and hearing of stories. Every single person in a church has a story, and we must create the opportunity for us to share those stories in safe settings, listening to one another:

- understanding where we came from,
- what energizes us and what empties us,
- what delights us and what defeats us, and
- what we are ashamed of and what we aspire to.

One of the most remarkable aspects of a thriving church is when our relationships go beyond what is natural or comfortable for us when we can connect with people across racial, gender, age, and socioeconomic divides. When you think about it, church is one of the only places in our culture where that is possible, where we have the potential to meet and know some folks we would never have crossed paths with otherwise.

In the early years of building Willow Creek, we rented spaces to meet for both our Sunday and midweek gatherings. I was a volunteer at the time, and our midweek service called "New Community" met for a while in the small auditorium of a local high school. Warren and I were by then seriously dating, so we sat together. During the turn-and-greet moment, we turned around and discovered a young African American guy with a huge grin. He introduced himself as Joe and quickly moved from the anticipated shaking of hands to a full-on hug. We told Joe our names, and then he asked, "Where do you live?" Warren owned a home near that school, and Joe wanted the address, saying he might stop by sometime.

Little did we know that God was launching a forty-year friendship in which Joe is a valued member of our extended family. Joe grew up near the church at a home for mentally and physically challenged kids. The state of Illinois placed him there after some foster care experiences that didn't work out well. Joe was a wiry kid, with more energy than I can describe, who rode his bike everywhere. He heard about Willow Creek and just boldly showed up.

Our friendship with Joe has been life changing for all of us. I believe God assigned us to each other. Joe has taught me more about childlike faith, bold prayers, and generosity to others than I have learned from books or professors or experts. And we got to help Joe find his way as an adult, get jobs and a place to live, and be there for him through several health challenges. There are times when we drive one another crazy. Joe never lets us know when he is going to drop by, and his timing is impeccable! When I'm most worn out and in need of downtime, there's a good chance Joe will blow into the house like a hurricane, picking me up in a bear hug, and scaring our little dog half to death. I know for sure that I never would have known Joe without the local church. Our love for Jesus brought us to that high school one summer night forty years ago, and now we are family. That is the wonder of community in the local church.

In his superb book *Analog Church*, Pastor Jay Y. Kim lays out how community forms us:

> Since its earliest days, the church has been about unlikely people gathering as family, in spite of their differences, living in uncomfortable community with one another, learning together to become one in the transformative presence and by the transformative power of Jesus Christ.

I believe that churches can be wobbly in a lot of ways—not so great at strategic planning, fundraising, or meeting in less-than-ideal settings—but if that church is built on a foundation of authentic community, it can thrive. Love makes up for a multitude of misses. Jesus told us the world will know we belong to him by how we love one another, how we walk with one another, how we forgive one another, how we show up for one another, how we listen to one another, how we believe the best about one another. I have tasted the wonder of community over and over again. That original group of arts leaders on my staff team worked together for more than twenty years. Now we are all in different churches but still in the Chicago area. We gather periodically—on my calendar it says "Old Buddies." We did life together and are still doing life together as we age and go through retirement challenges, health challenges, and the new joys of grandparenting for some.

I'm writing this chapter during the global pandemic of the early 2020s. Never have I missed gathering in community more! I long to hug my friends and linger over long meals and talk about what's happening in our lives. This week the old buddies did a Zoom call instead, and there was laughter and tears and lots of stories, even some confession. Holy moments of community. Not the same as gathering in a living room or around a kitchen table but the best we can do for now.

———

What does community look like for each generation? Are there fundamental differences in how we pursue, value, and live out this desire? I'm convinced that while we all desperately need to be known and loved, the forms and practical building of community may look and feel different for not only each generation but also for various cultures as well. How we seek and live out community may be only partly about our age and even more about our individual wiring and norms of our people groups. How community gets built is less important than whether it gets built at all. To varying degrees every human must fight the desires to isolate, hide, and battle life alone—and be willing to become part of the *We*.

Occasionally I imagine a few of my Generation X friends who are now in their forties, many of them leading churches. At some point a young group of millennials or Generation Z will ask for a meeting. They may describe changes they would like to see in the church to reach their generation. If they for a moment suggest that their longing for community is unique to them, my advice is to put a smile on your face, nod, and act as though they have come up with something new and essential for the church to thrive. Listen well to their hearts and minds without revealing your rising defensiveness. Seek to understand. Then you can excuse yourself and have a little screaming fit in the bathroom!

SAMANTHA

1-3-1-4 was the code to my old favorite place. You'd miss it if you weren't looking for it: a narrow hallway snaking through the underbelly of the church I grew up in. When the keypad signals its beeps of belonging, the door opens to a burst of laughter dancing down the hall, like a campfire promising warmth to a distant traveler. When I was little, I couldn't help but run toward it.

The Tunnel, as it was christened, was where my favorite people were: the artists. It served as a green room, rehearsal space, and kitchen, with a door *(1-3-5-7)* leading to a steep staircase winding up and onto the stage. The walls were littered with poster sheet blueprints full of circles, arrows, words, and images that had materialized into the creative elements of the service that was unfolding overhead. As a child there was nowhere I'd rather be, which is funny to think of now. There were rarely other people my age in the Tunnel. I didn't understand half of the jokes the drama team made, nor had I seen the *Seinfeld* episodes they were referencing. I just wanted to *be there*. To sit quietly at the table and soak in the togetherness of it all. It was in the Tunnel that I discovered the texture of community, what it felt like and sounded like. And though I couldn't name that at the time, I've been searching for it ever since.

Moving around a lot has made this challenging. As a single woman bouncing between big cities and too many roommates in too-small apartments, I was both empowered by independence and depressed by my anonymity. I remember one late New York City night walking to the train when I had the thought, *If I disappeared, it would take a long time for anyone to notice.*

Going to church in these new cities, I wanted somewhere I could belong above all else. I was floating between families—the one I was born into and the one I hoped to someday begin. I longed to inhabit a me-sized space in a community that would appreciate my presence and take notice of my absence. I wanted to walk into a room where I was known. This is hard to find in your twenties. There's no door code.

The church I attended in Brooklyn had interminable turn-and-greets. I'm not exaggerating; they had to be ten minutes long. I *like* talking to people (I can't imagine what this would have felt like for an introvert); that wasn't the problem. I put on what my friend Tamara and I call "open face": ready eyes, slight smile, open to the present moment. (We used this term to describe what people look like during their first month living in New York and why so many people talk to you on the subway if you're new or visiting. If you have a resting face of curiosity and wonderment, you are inviting these encounters. It becomes necessary over time to close your face a little. Some saintly people maintain a natural open face throughout their life, and you know immediately when you have met such a person. It feels like they have been waiting for you.)

At the Brooklyn church I had the most open of open faces as I turned in circles looking for someone to connect with. But Sunday after Sunday, people swarmed to greet the people they *knew*. It was more of a beeline and greet. Once all the smaller circles had formed I would aimlessly check my phone and wish that the service would get on with itself already. I grew to hate this part of the service and how it reminded me of my exclusion from what C. S. Lewis calls "the Inner Ring."

Eventually, I joined a "life group." I knew right away that I would get along with Tom. He'd spent his life in New York, doggedly pursuing a career in theater. He was in his sixties when we met. With a gravelly voice that seemed made for the stage, he'd tell tales from the Italian restaurant he worked in and the auditions he'd gone on that week. Tom didn't book many (any) of those auditions, but he never gave up.

Tom loves Jesus. He starts every day with an hour of prayer. One night I came to our small group particularly discouraged about a bad audition, wondering if I'd be working my terrible personal-assistant job forever, already on the verge of giving up after only a year of trying to make it as an actress. As we were sharing updates about our lives, Tom shared how grateful he was for Jesus' love: "I just can't believe how much he loves me. That he's forgiven me, that he wants to know me and walk with me. Anything that happens in my career is just a cherry on top. I already have the whole cake."

Eight years later I still think about those words when I encounter artistic disappointments or even victories. *I already have the whole cake.* In spiritual community we experience these shifts in perspective over and over. There is a limit to how much of God I can experience on my own. God's face shines through all faces, whether the world has taught them to remain open or closed. We just have to stick around long enough to notice.

On Sundays, when it came time for the turn-and-greet, I started to beeline for Tom.

———

My current church in Austin, Texas, sums up their approach to community and connection this way: if you want it, you gotta fight for it. The lean staff has grown weary of creating infrastructure, programming Bible studies, orchestrating dinners only for no one to show up. For attendance to start strong and then fade. For the very people who requested specific kinds of connection opportunities to forget to go, consumed by the thousands of other things we do in a week.

Our church's do-it-yourself fellowship approach makes it easy for people to stay on their islands. But people like Don and Terra will brave any sea to get to you.

This couple in their sixties arrives at church fifteen minutes early most weeks. They serve in many ways, but one is through this rigorous commitment to being present with those who may be new or alone. Visitors usually get to church before the lazy regulars, and Don and Terra make sure these newcomers have someone to talk to in those idle minutes before the place fills up and the music begins. They are warm and easy to connect with. In fact, Don might actually be Jesus—he is a carpenter and also a potter. Like a literal potter of clay. He has a ponytail. But most likely Don is just Don, and he and his wife are master includers.

I wonder what a church community would look like if more attention was given to discipleship in the art of including. I wonder how you teach people "open face."

It takes courage to dress up, ride the train, walk the blocks, find which part of the school has been turned into a sanctuary, sit alone, and fill out an info card. It's even more daring to sign up for a small group, buy cookies, get on a bus, find an address, realize you've forgotten a gluten-free option, press a buzzer, announce your name knowing it carries no meaning, sit on a stranger's couch, discover this was more of a wine thing than a cookie thing, and then abruptly disclose matters of the heart. And I'm a White, straight, extroverted pastor's daughter! I love meeting new people. I know the language. I don't fear rejection, not really.

What is being asked of someone whose experience with the church has taught them they are not welcome? What must someone risk to discover whether or not they can belong in your community of faith? For those who the church has historically marginalized and oppressed, how can your church communicate that they will be safe in your living rooms? Do you know if they actually will be?

In her book *Native,* Kaitlin Curtice writes of her experience navigating White church spaces as an Indigenous woman: "The older I get, the more I realize how wired I am for community, for relationship, for belonging. Sadly, the church isn't always that place."

It took a long time before I understood that Tom was gay. He often used vague language about wrestling with God over parts of his identity. Another friend from our group remembers it like this: "I felt like he was always taking our temperature as a group on how we would react."

That space, which I grew to feel so comfortable returning to week after week and sharing what felt like my most vulnerable confessions, did not feel safe to Tom. What had I done to make it this way? What assumptions had we made? What could we have done differently to ensure that every part of every one of us was welcome? These questions haunt me still.

My academic husband, Will, had a lot of resistance to church culture when we were dating. He believed in God but didn't want to check his brain at the door. Thinking it might be good for him to get to know other men of faith, I convinced him to join a small group for the first time in his life.

It did not go well.

At the *very first* session of the *very first* small group, the *very first* question asked by the leader was, "So, do you side more with God or science?" Will never went back.

Research professor Brené Brown sums it up: "True community is where no one has to hide."

———

A 2019 poll by YouGov verified that millennials have surpassed Generation X and baby boomers as the loneliest generation. And that was before the global pandemic that forced the not-yet-marrieds and not-yet-settled to hunker down in isolation for a year and counting. The Cigna Loneliness Index survey released in 2020 found 71 percent of millennials and nearly 79 percent of Generation Z report feeling lonely—a significant uptick from previous generations.

Can our collective ache for community be met by the local church?

In response to frustrations with my notoriously flaky generation, some churches have tried to gather us "young folks" where we already are: the internet. They put all their efforts into assembling online communities and conversations. During Covid-19, this has been the only form of connection many of us could have, and I am grateful for it. But while the virtual world provides us with tools, I'm unconvinced that our avatars can ever fulfill our bodies' deepest longings.

When it does become safe to gather again, I wonder if the local church will continue to try to outrun one of its most distinctive features: its localness! Millennials are changing residences more than any other generation (every two years, on average, according to a study from Porch). Is the church on the corner a physical space we can walk into and find warmth in a new place? For us untethered ones, if the church nearby offers a true, inclusive, embracing, authentic, vibrant, three-dimensional community, that would be deeply compelling if not irresistible.

A few years after Rev. Rebecca Anderson and Rev. Vince Amlin started Gilead Church in Chicago, their team identified loneliness as a problem they could help address. They began throwing huge parties—epic, beautiful, and open to all. They threw a catered dinner on the "L" train, an Easter dance party. "It was the kind of thing that might get a total stranger to come," Anderson says. "And it did." Now it's become one of their core practices and worked its way into their mission statement: *a community that makes beautiful worship, throws great parties, and tells true stories that save lives.* People come for the parties and stay for the church.

At the time I am writing this, my husband and I are in the process of buying our first house. Neither of us is what I would call handy, and when we fell in love with a house built in 1949, we called Don to take a look at it with us. He walked through it carefully, speaking the language of electricity and plumbing with our inspector. He followed up a few days later to recommend an electrician (three actually, each with a personal story) and to give his feedback on the house, which he framed as parental ("you gotta know what you're getting into"). Here, in the middle of Texas, so far away from family or anyone we would ask to help us with such an enormous decision, Will and I had a parent in Don.

I believe the intergenerational aspect of church community is deeply undervalued. Most churches siphon off community groups according to age and season of life. But where else can folks my age find a Don? In Brooklyn I remember how good it felt to hold a baby, to sit at a family dinner table with non-Ikea furniture, to listen to Tom's stories. In Chicago I loved volunteering with student ministry, where young people start to ask real, hard questions and everybody's trying to figure out who they are. Our stories might not intersect if not for the local church.

I have so many memories of my mom and her friends—artists, volunteers, and members of our church—being *with* one another. Laughing and creating in the Tunnel, gathered in our living room, around a table, Christmas parties, funerals, graduations, births, and hospital beds. I remember them *showing up* for one another over and over and over—for the peaks and valleys and all the meals to be eaten in between. I call them my aunts and uncles. They were, and are, a family.

I seriously wonder if I will have that someday.

Sometimes I try to return to the Tunnel, but it's like they've changed the code on me. What was the magic? What made that so special? How was it that all those people wanted to be in the same place at the same time? Why weren't they distracted? Why did I want to be there so badly (besides that it might remind the drama director that I was around, in case, you know, he needed me for any upcoming roles)?

I'm waiting for community to happen to me as it happened to Mom. But maybe it won't happen on my terms or my schedule. Maybe she chose it. Again and again.

When it comes to community, I imagine that I and my mom and her mom and all generations before us wanted something similar. How we get there might shift, but I don't think the goal has: to be seen and loved. To break free of what Barbara Brown Taylor calls "the prison of yourself" and be transformed by the face of God in others.

I want wisdom about parenting from people farther down the road, and I want to celebrate young people who are headed off to college. I want to get in the car after we leave someone's house and say, "I'm glad we went" instead of "I didn't know how to leave" because our whole selves showed up, not because I put on a good show. I want people at my dinner table who I would never meet if it weren't for the church. I want someone to call when Texas freezes over and I'm not sure what to do about our pipes. I want someone to call me and share the creative dreams they're afraid to speak out loud. I want to be yanked out of my regular programming to meet Jesus in the people I least expect. I want to talk (and not just think) about inequity in my city and practice (and not just post about) justice work. When loss throws my world upside down, I want people to sit near me, to pray for me when I can't remember how. And I want to participate in these fragments of other people's lives because consuming them through a screen costs me nothing and transforms me even less.

There are many things a church can do to make it *easier* to show up. Interrogate the language of the culture and the unwritten code of belonging. Consider who it excludes. Train up more Dons and Terras. Lead with love rather than beliefs (especially in small-group icebreakers). And take notice that those of us who've been marketed to our entire lives might gravitate more toward connection opportunities designed around serving rather than reading the pastor's book together.

But at the end of the day I am the only one who can make sure I arrive. I am convicted by these words in Noreena Hertz's book *The Lonely Century*, and I think one could easily substitute the word *society* with the word *church*:

> Because society isn't only done to us, we "do" society too, we participate in it and shape it. So if we want to stop the destructive path of loneliness and restore the sense of community and cohesion we have lost, we will need to acknowledge that there are steps we must take, as well as tradeoffs we will have to make—between individualism and collectivism, between self-interest and societal good, between anonymity and familiarity, between convenience and caring, between what is right for the self and what is best for the community, between liberty and fraternity.

It seems the deep and diverse community I long for will cost me my comfort. My infatuation with ease. All of me will have to show up instead of the carefully curated image I'd rather send on my behalf. I will have to offer the one thing nearly every other aspect of modern life is helping me to preserve: time. I must also interrogate my wanderlust, nurtured by advertising and stories that taught me to desire exploration, novelty, and adventure. It is the antithesis of the invitation to *dwell*. The church has the potential to remind us that we were created for life *with* one another, messy, slow, and inefficient as it may be.

———

Will and I are putting down roots. We bought the house, after all. (Don's going to help us build a porch!) We know a few folks at our new church, though the pandemic has kept us at a distance. I wonder what will happen next.

We might pass through each other, tourists sharing a beach for a summer.

Or maybe we'll tie our boats together and embark on something better.

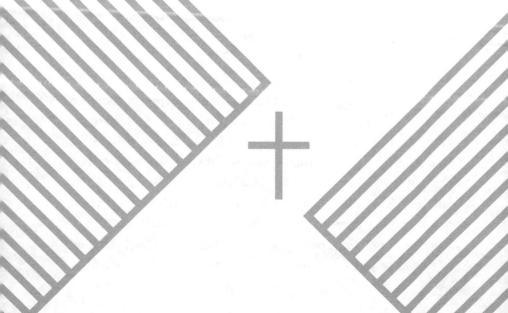

2

Train Up a Child in the Way She Should Go, and She Will Never Forget the Hand Motions

Being Kidcentric

NANCY

"Hey, Janet, stop for a second," I called out to my best friend and next-door neighbor. Janet was ahead of me as we rode our bicycles home on a hot day in June after attending Vacation Bible School at my church. Janet likely thought something was wrong with my bike until I surprised her with a question. "Do you want to do it?"

"Do what?" she asked.

"You know, pray that prayer they taught us about today, asking Jesus to be our Savior and to forgive us?"

"Sure, I guess so," was her tentative response. So we leaned our little bikes up against one of the tall maple trees on Prospect Avenue and bowed our heads to pray out loud together. I was seven years old. That moment launched me into a lifelong relationship with Jesus. Forty years later, when I was forty-seven, I drove back to Park Ridge, a sleepy suburb of Chicago near O'Hare Airport. I parked my car in front of the little house where I lived through elementary school and walked about three blocks toward the church of my youth. I had no idea what exact tree we had chosen for the moment of prayer, but about halfway through my walk I stopped and reflected on how my decision four decades prior had marked me forever.

South Park Church, a nondenominational community of faith, became a second home to my family and me. I knew the building inside and out, including the winding and musty back staircase built of wood so dark it bordered on black, hidden behind the stage of the old gymnasium where we lined up for relay races. I can still see the pristinely clean tiled hallways with tiny rooms for Sunday school, the overpass connecting the old building and the new, the ivory pews in the sanctuary, with walls painted a pale blue color resembling bird eggs, the tall windows lining both sides, letting in rays of sunshine and warmth. Our life seemed to revolve around morning and evening church but also midweek events such as Pioneer Girls (a Christian version of Girl Scouts). I loved going to church—it was a safe and fun place for me. I marvel now at how many adults invested volunteer time with the children. There was Mrs. Christenson, who told me what it meant to choose to follow Jesus. Mr. Gottschalk, a large man with an infectious laugh, affected me with his contagious joy. At children's church Mr. Ernie sought to instill in us a love for memorizing Scripture by turning it into an intense competition that included prizes selected from a catalog of riches! When I was the winner, I chose a new plaid jumper to add to my wardrobe.

Mrs. Sauter was assigned to be my "pal" in Pioneer Girls, which meant she served as a sort of mentor, though we didn't use that word back then. Mrs. Jorian, who had eight children of her own, became a pseudo-mother to me, always willing to talk and inviting us to hang out in her kidcentric basement, complete with a ping-pong table and comfy floor pillows. I hold treasured memories of parties there that featured lots of yummy food like toasted ham-and-cheese sandwiches, chips, and all kinds of soda pop that we didn't have at my house. Then there was Mrs. Cousins, the one who pierced my ears, and her best friend, Mrs. Horgan. To this day I am unable to call these adults—now in their eighties and nineties or already in heaven—by their first names. Except for one: Char. She was my oh-so-cool Sunday school teacher my freshman year who ended up being a friend and mentor for life until she passed away a few years ago. Char was like an adult hippie who dressed in boho full skirts and strappy sandals, wore her hair long and straight, and allowed us to talk about absolutely anything. Char, a full-time writer, seemed exotic to me. She insisted we call her Char even though she was the same age as our parents. Most importantly, Char displayed a simple love of Jesus that made me want to love him too.

God does some of his most magnificent work in and through children, through the little ones. It was the children of South Park Church in the early 1970s who unknowingly joined the birth of a movement. When I was fifteen years old, two new youth leaders arrived at that little church—Dave Holmbo and Bill Hybels. Dave came first to lead us musically and later to build an arts ministry that unleashed all kinds of creative arts, including multimedia on the screen, drama sketches, dance, visual arts, and, of course, contemporary music. I distinctly remember the night Bill Hybels arrived on his Harley Davidson motorcycle. He was only twenty but a powerful force even back then. I could not possibly have foreseen how this leader would shape my future, ignite my gifts, and later hurt me and others with his abuse of power and inappropriate relationships with women.

Our youth group up until the era of Bill and Dave consisted of about thirty students meeting in the basement of the church singing songs like "Pass It On." Bill began experimenting with a newly discovered gift for teaching, and we approached the Bible with a childlike earnestness and faith, actually believing it might be true. God stirred in us a genuine love for our friends at school who did not yet know Jesus. Under the leadership of Bill and Dave, we designed a new experience to reach our friends, calling it Son City Spectacular. (We eventually dropped *Spectacular*, perhaps discerning it was a little over the top.) By the time I was a senior in high school, that youth group had exploded miraculously to over twelve hundred students, dwarfing the number of adults at the church. We identified with the early Christians in Acts 2, who were filled with awe and who saw many people joining the family of God. I got to be a part of leading a friend—my biology partner from school—to faith in Jesus.

In 1975 Bill and Dave followed a leading from God to leave that youth ministry, move about twenty-five miles west, and launch a church called Willow Creek in a movie theater. Some of us who were at the center of the South Park youth ministry became founders of that church and movement. I don't believe this was a coincidence but a result of God sowing seeds in us from our childhood and the investment of all the adults, including Pastor LeRoy Patterson (who taught me it was okay to laugh in church) and Pastor Arthur Evans Gay (a man of great integrity and wisdom who still speaks into my life today).

We know that Jesus held children in high regard, rebuking his disciples when they tried to keep the little ones away from him. Instead, Jesus gently placed his hands on the children and prayed for them, saying, "Let the little children come to me, and do not hinder them, for the kingdom of heaven belongs to such as these" (Matthew 19:14). One chapter earlier, in Matthew 18, Jesus taught that unless we adults become childlike, we cannot enter the kingdom of heaven. We must humble ourselves and adopt the curiosity, openness, faith, trust, delight, and wonder of the little ones.

Just as I was positively marked by loving adults in my home and my little church who pointed me toward the love and joy of Jesus, I know others carry a strikingly different story. Many adults struggle with the concept of a loving heavenly Father or a healthy church community because of experiences in their youth marked by apathy, racism, overbearing rules, punishment, and in some cases abuse. I first met Jennifer when she came to Chicago to be a part of one of my coaching circles for women in leadership. (This account includes the story of her abuse; if you'd prefer to skip it, you can skip ahead about three pages.)

Jennifer immediately stood out as the only one in the circle with an armful of tattoos and purple and red streaks in her long, dark hair. I couldn't wait to hear her story. Jennifer, now fifty-one, loves Jesus and leads a beautiful ministry to those with disabilities as well as a recovery ministry at her church. Given the abuse she experienced from several church leaders when she was just twelve years old, it's a modern-day miracle that Jennifer would ever return to God and a community of faith.

Jennifer is a Southern California native. Her first encounter with abuse began when she was eight. Her mother was diagnosed with multiple sclerosis, which had already propelled her to fits of anger that resulted in beatings for Jennifer and her three siblings. With an emotionally distant father, the home was volatile. They did go to church regularly, and it became a haven for Jennifer. She loved the youth group and singing in the choir. Before she was twelve, Jennifer says that little church was "like heaven" to her.

Then one day a man who cleaned the church building invited Jennifer to his home next door to the church to hang out with his family before the Wednesday evening meetings. This man was a stepfather to some children who were in the kitchen. He invited Jennifer to come with him into the living room, where the television was blaring, asking her to sit on his lap. He began molesting Jennifer, and she froze, not knowing what to do. She prayed for God to help her. One of the other children came into the room and told the stepfather the garbage disposal had broken in the kitchen. He left to fix it, leaving Jennifer hoping all was done—but then he sent the other kids outside and started inappropriately touching her again. The television blew out, which led him to take her hand to go into the bedroom. As Jennifer stood, there was a knock at the door, saying they had to get back to church for choir practice. Jennifer believes God rescued her at that moment from any further abuse. She walked into choir practice acting as if nothing happened.

Over the next few weeks Jennifer's demeanor completely changed. Her joy and delight were replaced with edginess and anger. She started telling people that Jesus is a fraud and the church is full of hypocrites. One of the youth leaders, a woman, suspected that maybe something had happened to trigger this abrupt transformation. She gently asked Jennifer some probing questions, and after a while the truth came out. A meeting was set up in the senior pastor's office. The five people in the meeting included that pastor, two very young youth leaders (including the woman), and the man who was the perpetrator. The pastor told Jennifer to sit in the chair next to the man accused and then asked the man first what happened. He reported that two times Jennifer had brushed up against him indicating she wanted more, putting all the blame on the twelve-year-old girl. The pastor didn't ask Jennifer any questions at all. He said that because there was no intercourse, Jennifer should not tell her parents and that he would provide counseling to this man. He told Jennifer to stay away from the guy and his family, and that was that.

Almost forty years later Jennifer still gets uncomfortable describing the moment. The meeting was almost worse than the molesting. She was not heard or believed or protected in any way. For the next eighteen years Jennifer ran as far away from God and church as she could, using drugs and alcohol to try to escape from the pain of her home and her church. She no longer felt safe anywhere.

Most stories like Jennifer's don't have a happy ending. But when Jennifer was thirty, a friend invited her to a different church. She had huge doubts that the pastor who was preaching could be the real thing. She got up the courage to send him an email and tell him the story of what happened to her at age twelve. They began to exchange emails, and finally one day they met. Jennifer lobbed a challenge at the pastor, saying, "I loved Jesus at twelve. Give me a reason to love him now." Over the next days, weeks, and years Jennifer returned to God and this family of faith where she now serves on full-time staff as a wounded healer, coming alongside others who are broken. Recently Jennifer completed her second master's degree, this one a master of divinity. She is still finding healing in a counseling relationship, knowing she was marked forever by the trauma she experienced as a child. Jennifer is truly one of my heroes. Her story is both a cautionary tale and a testament to God's magnificent grace.

Jesus didn't just have nice things to say about children. He also fiercely protected them and lambasted anyone who might cause them harm. Look at these strong words: "Whoever welcomes a little child like this in my name welcomes me. If anyone causes one of these little ones—those who believe in me—to stumble, it would be better for them to have a large millstone hung around their neck and to be drowned in the depths of the sea" (Matthew 18:5-6).

When we consider the influence adults can have for either good or evil on the impressionable hearts and minds of the young, we ought to quake in our shoes.

━━

When I became a mom, I was on the staff of what became known as one of the megachurches. I wondered what my daughters' experiences of church would look like in contrast to my childhood at a much smaller church where so many people knew my name. Willow Creek called the children's ministry Promiseland, and for many years it was led by the visionary Sue Miller, who is also one of my closest friends. Sue and her team reimagined what Sunday school could be for the little ones, and they were determined to make the experience the best hour of a kid's week. When Samantha was about four years old, there were many months when she would only wear one outfit to

Promiseland—her Minnie Mouse dress! Her earliest teachers, like Mr. Duane, would smile to see her bouncing in week after week with her black and red polka dots.

My girls did not experience Bible-memory competition like I did (or flannel-board Bible stories either). But they did come away with the most significant of big ideas: that there is a God who loves them with a boundless, outrageous love; that they were created as a unique person with special gifts to discover; that the most remarkable news is that while we are all sinners, there is a Savior who wants to forgive us; that we should love all people no matter what; that words like "I'm sorry" are essential; that the Bible is the Word of God on which we can build our lives. I now understand more clearly how vital it is for parents to know the church is a partner in the spiritual development of little ones, to know that we are not alone, to be blessed with a few other adults who become a part of the village that raises a child.

Research from both the Barna Group and the International Bible Society reveals that a large majority of people who ever become a Christian do so before the age of eighteen. The Barna study showed that two out of three (64 percent) made a commitment to follow Christ before their eighteenth birthday. The findings of the Bible Society were even more staggering, revealing that 83 percent of all Christians made their first commitment to Jesus between the ages of four and fourteen (called the *4/14 window*). When my friend Sue Miller and other advocates of children's ministry see these statistics, they want to shout from the rooftops, "Then why aren't churches investing a hugely disproportionate amount of resources into children's ministry?" Great question.

It's almost a cliché that often young couples who haven't been regular church attenders for years decide to find a church once they have children. Maybe they want to offer their little ones something that meant more to them in their past, even if they would not describe themselves as committed Christ-followers. I firmly believe that going forward, churches must elevate their focus on ministry to children, students, and families.

Many people in the United States grew up with some experience of church as a child or high school student, and yet statistics show us that a large majority now identify with the Nones in terms of religious affiliation. The "Great Opportunity" report tells us that over forty million young people who were raised in Christian homes could walk away from a life with Jesus by 2050. Half the young people who grew up in church have already left. This sobering trend goes beyond the facts to real people, real families who wonder if their prodigal sons and daughters will ever come back to faith and the church. Some of my baby boomer friends raised their children the same way we did, lovingly guiding their children at home, and yet they are mourning the choices their now-young-adult kids have made to abandon the faith or at least to abandon church. Perhaps one of the promises clung to most often in Scripture by parents is found in Proverbs 22:6: "Start children off on the way they should go, and even when they are old they will not turn from it."

Clearly, from experience this doesn't always seem to hold true for everyone, or at least the evidence makes us doubt its truth. I pray regularly for these young adults by name who have wandered, wondering if their parents will ever see them come home to God. One story in my extended family gives me hope for the promise. It is the story of my father's path to God and faith.

———

My Great-Aunt Ellen arrived at Ellis Island as a teenager, an immigrant from Sweden, in about 1918. She moved to Chicago with her younger brother. Ellen never married, but she was involved in the lives of her three nephews, including my father, Warren (yes, my father and my husband are both named Warren).

My dad and his brothers grew up during the Great Depression in a small tenement apartment on the south side of Chicago, and my father's parents were not people of faith and did not go to church. My grandfather was an alcoholic, and the family struggled financially. Aunt Ellen invited my father and his brothers to go to church with her. The other two boys showed no interest, but my dad went often. He remembers sitting in Sunday school in a little red chair, learning the song "Jesus Loves Me." My dad did not commit to faith in Jesus as a boy, but a seed had been sown. Much later, in his late twenties, Dad did become a believer, no doubt remembering from his youth that Jesus loved him. He was a fighter pilot in World War II and also in the Korean War.

After both wars my parents settled in the suburbs and began attending South Park Church, where my faith was launched. Do you see the ripple effect going back to my Aunt Ellen? My father passed away several years ago at ninety-two. In his final days, when he could no longer talk, we would sing to him. I am a terrible singer, but when I was alone in his hospital room, I would sing songs of the faith. And his favorite, the one that made his blue eyes twinkle, was "Jesus Loves Me." At the memorial service for Dad, we told the story of Aunt Ellen and the little red chair. Samantha was on a flight back home after the funeral, and she wrote a poem titled "The Little Red Chair." She describes all the different kinds of chairs my dad sat on in his life, including his chair as a pilot and the big cushy chair he sat in as he grew old. She also mentions his very short engagement of just six days to my mom before he headed to WWII.

In a little red chair a little boy sat
where Aunt Ellen had dropped him

until she would return.
In a little red chair, a little boy learned
"Jesus Loves Me."
That's what he was told:
"Jesus loves me, this I know."
This he came to know
the boy
in the chair
and he sang along to his new favorite song
because singing it might make it true.
And because it's by far
The Most Catchy
of all the songs that were taught
to red chairs in those days.
Was his voice hollow even then?
A little boy with my grandfather's voice:
"Little ones to him belong,"
lifting up little voices from little red chairs.
Not knowing anything of
the chairs to come.
At the Illinois Institute of Numbers,
where he'd work to study
and study to work
and sit in a stiff chair
and prove that he knew
enough to sit in a cockpit,
a small chair, a severe chair
with a dangerous view entrusted to him—
a chair he'd probably only know the edge of
like the wooden pews he'd barely touch,
giddy as he'd be
when he'd say "I do"

to a woman he barely knew!
But would sit with
in movie theater seats, at booths, on benches, car seats,
    and couches,
in waiting room chairs and upon kitchen stools
for sixty-eight years to come.
His chair at the table with three girls and a son
His seat behind the wheel on a sticky road trip
Folding chairs at the receptions of the weddings of his babies
Hospital chairs where he'd first hold the babies of his babies
A padded seat in the dining room of a retirement buffet
Until finally,
a light blue chair
that slightly sways
from which he will watch whatever sport is in season
next to his bride. Who has never not been in season.
But he didn't know of this then!
Singing boldly from the first chair
Because Aunt Ellen told him to
Because the Bible told him so
Is this then what is meant
by a legacy of faith?
Someone called Aunt Ellen
sat a little boy in a little red chair
and he learned "Jesus Loves Me."
Yes, Jesus loves me,
and he sang it right from there
until he knew it by heart
and could sing it from any chair
he would occupy.
Because singing it, he found it to be true.
And so he would sing it to his babies in their high chairs.

And they would sing it to their babies in their car seats.
And they would all sing it back to him
when he could no longer
Sit
Up
But this he knew. Jesus loves me. Yes, yes, yes.
Even now
Aunt Ellens drop kids in little red chairs
and Grandpa sings their song before a big red throne.

Even now children experience the equivalent of little red chairs—vivid memories of a place and of people who let them know, week after week, that Jesus loves them. I have to believe those sown seeds matter and that every community of faith should be a place where the little ones are welcomed, protected, and deeply loved.

SAMANTHA

Showing up to Promiseland was like arriving at my own birthday party every weekend. The way the leaders and volunteers greeted me felt like they'd been waiting just for me so that church could finally start. I was whisked away to an experience completely unlike any other part of my week: every Promiseland service was full of live music, dance, drama, games, and teaching by gifted communicators who I found very funny and cool. A church is always sending messages (the *subtext*, as we call it in theater), and the very first memo I got from my very first church was, *there is a place for you here.*

There is no second chance at first impressions. I love God now in large part because I met him in Promiseland.

Promiseland was the name for the kids' ministry I grew up in—and for a child like me who longed to visit Oz, Narnia, and Terabithia—it was a far more compelling place to visit than "Willow Creek Kids" would have been. Names matter. And Promiseland was a destination, not a daycare.

We always went to the Saturday night service (so my mom and her team could do a debrief and make changes before Sunday), which meant that if I was lucky, I could score both pizza and a sleepover following the service. Church rocked!

Still, something shifted when I joined the Promiseland drama team. There was a music team too, although I saw the writing on the wall early on: I was no Amy Grant. But maybe, just maybe, I could be a Deanna Armentrout.

You can always hear Deanna before you see her. Her vibrant life force is a thing to behold. She can, and does, cry at the drop of a hat (signaling to me that she was a "real" actress). She is a storyteller, the kind whose stories were *so* fantastic they were requested by name. She is a tremendous listener (the *true* mark of a real actress). And she was the director of the Promiseland drama team.

On this team I received regular and intensive acting training, *and* we performed short drama scenes for different age groups in Promiseland that were carefully crafted to help bring that weekend's message to life. I played a crabby kid on Christmas in a scene that preceded teaching on gratitude. I played a superhero in a service about battling the negative voices in your head. I did a rap about searching for truth. I got to participate in the programming for my peers, and that changed everything.

Now, I was getting new messages from the church: *Your gifts matter to God. Your friends matter to God. There is great joy in serving—and doing it with excellence.*

Deanna and her team believed all of the extra effort that working with kids entails—the complex scheduling, dealing with parents, time, parents, money, parents—was worth it to empower kids to serve in their own ministry. They believed that kids seeing other kids onstage would resonate with kids in a way that adults just couldn't. They believed it wasn't too early for us to get serious about developing our creative gifts, and they believed those gifts could serve the church. After ten years on the Promiseland drama team (in high school, they taught me to direct and teach), I think they were right.

My husband, Will, is an educator with a particular passion for student-driven learning. There is ample research that tells us how much more effective learning environments are when participants are actively engaged in the curriculum. Student-centered learning embraces the idea that we learn better when we are participants, not merely consumers of our education, and when we see ourselves represented.

When Will was a child, on his first day of Christian school, each student was asked to recite their favorite verse. He couldn't think of any and still remembers the teacher's shock and students' laughter. A few years later he remembers being told that the Jewish girl he was crushing on was going to hell. And, as a child of divorce, he didn't understand why his youth-group friend wasn't allowed to come over and play at his mom's house.

These early encounters with Christian community are formative—for better or worse. Twenty years later Will wanted to believe in God but struggled to reconcile the message of love with his first experiences of the church that were marked by shame. Will tiptoed through the doors of a church at age twenty-six, guarded and rightly suspicious. The message he had received: *you might not fit here.*

We have a reputation for drawing lines around our God who promises there's nowhere he isn't. Too often rules and judgment define youth ministry as if we can somehow indoctrinate a ten-year-old into a lifetime of safe friends and smart choices. Though my early church experience was overwhelmingly constructive, there was still the evangelical undergirding of good news for some and bad news for the rest. "We have good news *if* . . ." And I attended enough Christian summer camps and have since sifted through enough church baggage with friends to wonder how fear became one of the fundamental tools for shaping young faith.

I prayed my first prayer of salvation at age four. I was very theologically advanced. It was after a Promiseland service about Satan. Okay, maybe the service wasn't *about* Satan (my mom insists that wasn't part of the curriculum for the four- and five-year-olds), but they mentioned him enough to stress me out. I was a big rule follower and, from what I understood, this Satan character could really make things difficult. I couldn't sleep (Satan dreams are the *worst*), and my dad sat with me and told me that with Jesus on my team I didn't have to be afraid.

When I got older and learned my spiritual ABCs (admit, believe, choose), I worried that my prayer hadn't followed that exact sequence. I was only four after all. So I prayed this magic prayer every year in Promiseland, again in middle school, and on several high school retreats. Everyone talked about it so much I wanted to make sure I had it down. As a young actress I very much understood the importance of getting my words right. It would really suck to not get into heaven because I dropped one of my lines. If the angels do have a book, my name is in there a lot.

"All afternoon activities are canceled. Report to the gymnastics gym immediately." This was a particular bummer on that hot Tuesday in July when I was supposed to enjoy a camp afternoon of archery, sailing, and free swim. Instead, I joined two hundred other tweens in a sticky gym to learn that the last prophecy had fallen into place and Jesus was on his way back. Possibly tonight, but no one seemed quite sure what flight he was on.

The camp director was an expert on the Holy Land and did know quite a lot about the book of Revelation and the geography of Israel. Checking them off on a whiteboard she marched through a series of prophecies and check marks, parts of the Bible that I had not previously known existed. I began to picture the book of Revelation like the Hall of Prophecy in the Harry Potter series, with thousands of dusty orbs, now shattering as the voices of the prophets rung out. By the end of the hour she had me and my cabin convinced we may never see our family and friends again. If Jesus' return was imminent, I needed to get out of there! I had business to attend to, people to hug, a room to clean, and a dog to convert (unsure as I was about Murphy's eternal destination). Astute readers will take note that Jesus did not return in the summer of 2002. But I spent the rest of camp in a panic.

In my teenage years Christian communities taught me of all that could not be trusted: the future, secular music, my body, secular books, different faiths, secular movies, and perhaps most of all—my own experience.

I can only imagine the fear parents endure as they prepare and release their child into the world, with all its great and terrible possibilities. I understand the appeal of a religious ecosystem that renders potential danger zones completely off-limits.

But between my purity contract (a contract I understood to be my first legal commitment: to refrain from sex until marriage), my anxieties regarding the magic prayer, Jesus coming back, my friends all being destined for hell, the serious responsibility of me and my one-piece to protect all guys from lust and stumbling, and music on the radio potentially corrupting my thoughts, being in church as a teenager was becoming very stressfull! My faith was suddenly full of land mines.

When I got to college I felt unprepared for the *questions*. Questions lobbed in dorm rooms by my new friends with different beliefs. Questions that sprung up in my soul. Questions that felt like they had the power to tear down the whole thing. *Where do we find permission to disregard certain commands in the Bible and uphold the rest? What about the violence, genocide, and rape condoned by the seemingly vengeful God of the Old Testament? How did the Bible come to be, anyway? How could a loving God "perfectly and wonderfully make" my LGBTQ+ friends and then demand a life of celibacy? Why don't boys wear purity rings? We sing about freedom, so why do I feel like I'm suffocating? Why does salvation feel so transactional? How can we trust in God's providence when so many are starving? Would a loving God banish millions of people to eternal torture? What about people of other faiths? What if I had been born into a different zip code and therefore a different faith tradition? If I weren't me, would this still be good news?* Certainly, some spiritual communities do engage thoughtfully with these questions, but they had not been addressed in my own church experience at that point.

I don't think it's such a mystery why young people abandon church in college or young adulthood. These are the years when our relational world expands beyond those we grew up with, our surroundings change, we learn critical thinking, and our worldview is exposed for what it is: *our* worldview. We learn that others' experience of our God and our Bible has been hurtful. We wonder if God can be trusted. All while we're learning to cook and do laundry! It's a lot.

So, the question becomes, Do you remember church as a place that was comfortable with mystery, paradox, and complexity? Do you remember church primarily as a force of love or as a system of beliefs? And if you tiptoed through the doors of a new church in a new city, would there be room for your doubts? Or would you sit through sixty minutes of people professing their rightness?

I see this expanding framework happening even earlier for the Gen Z high school students I work with in a summer theater program. Growing up with social media and 24-7 news has exposed them to the world outside their hometown before they ever have to leave it. Every year, without fail, they end up teaching me. They teach me how smart they are. How engaged. How compassionate. They teach me not to underestimate them. These kids won't settle for Christianese to explain away the unanswerable.

I know now that questions don't threaten God. But they sure do seem to threaten some student-ministry leaders. I sat in a lot of cross-legged circles throughout my teenage years and remember very few leaders who felt comfortable leaving questions unanswered. Letting them breathe. Saying "I don't know." Admitting that some of these answers aren't in the Bible.

If the best message a church can send a child is *you belong here*, I wonder if a meaningful memo to teens would be *you belong here and so does your voice.* What would it mean for youth groups to cultivate an appetite for mystery? To welcome doubt and introduce it as a friendly traveler on our faith journey? What would there be room for if we scaled back the disproportionate emphasis on evangelism and sex? How might student ministries lay a foundation for what Miroslav Volf and Lisa Sharon Harper call a "thick gospel" rather than a "thin faith" that "skims the surface of sacred texts, using what seems applicable in the moment without connecting the dots"? And how can shame be ruthlessly eradicated from a young person's experience of church?

When eleven-year-old Taylor told me she couldn't fall asleep, I pulled her out onto the front porch of our cabin to talk. We were only a few days into her session, so we didn't know each other well yet, but I'd already formed an impression of her. Funny, extroverted, athletic, and kind, Taylor had no problem making friends and seemed to love being at camp. But she couldn't look at me on the porch steps as she finally emptied the weight of her truth, the reason she was still awake.

"Sometimes, at night, I hear the devil telling me to do things."

"Okay . . . ," I said, buying time.

But no amount of extra minutes was going to help me arrive at a counselor-ly response to this kind of confession. I was nineteen! This wasn't part of our training! I knew all the camp cheers, how to teach breast stroke, and what to do for chigger bites—I was even good with homesick kids—but devil stuff was out of my element. (I conquered Satan at age four, remember?)

I asked a few follow-up questions. Her answers assured me she wasn't thinking of hurting herself or anyone else. But she was truly terrified of this voice and its power over her. I went inside to get my Bible, really needing my co-counselor (a *junior* in college and in my mind much more equipped for Satan stuff) to be awake—but she wasn't. Apparently, the devil didn't talk to her. Grabbing my Bible I thumbed through my brain's card catalog of whatever stories and verses had stuck. The only devil story I could think of was something about pigs. Not helpful! Back on the porch I stumbled through a random assortment of verses, prayed for her, and soon as she seemed calm, I sent her back to bed.

I did not sleep for one minute.

The whole night I stared at her bunk across the room from mine. I tried to tell myself the whole thing was absurd while every time she rolled over I half expected to see red eyes gleaming.

I learned that night that I didn't know what I believed about the devil. I'd heard of spiritual warfare but kind of thought that was just code for suffering as a Christian. Maybe this was just the voice in her head. Should I tell her that? Oh, that voice that's telling you to take one more cookie? That's not the devil. It's just *temptation*. That's what we call it. Don't worry, Taylor! Very common! But don't call it the devil again. At least not around here.

The next day I brought it up to the girls' camp director, Mrs. Freed. I connected her with Taylor, and they started spending time together during Taylor's free periods. I would see them walking and talking together. Taylor didn't have any more bad nights, at least as far as I could tell. This was officially *not my problem* anymore.

I realize now that it didn't matter what I believed about the devil. What mattered was whether or not I believed Taylor. Mrs. Freed did. She took her seriously. She took her problem seriously and her questions too. No doubt, Mrs. Freed had her own questions about devil stuff, and they seemed to be asking them together. Taylor wasn't alone. When she left camp, we informed her parents so they could connect her to a real-world counselor with the expertise we didn't have.

I wish I could go back to that night on the porch. I wish I knew that *having answers* wasn't the most important part of my job as a youth-ministry leader. I wish I would have said, "That must be really scary." I wish I would have known the ministry was simply sitting together, holding space for the terrifying, the true, and the unresolvable.

———

God has always been bigger than the box I tried to put him in. The older I get, the bigger God grows, overstepping so many of the boundaries I was taught he stayed inside of, showing up in the faces of those I learned were "lost." If you are raised in the church, your introduction to God and his Word is mediated by human beings. Limited, biased, goodhearted humans. The more of the world I become exposed to, the more of God I am starting to see. Brian McLaren speaks to the stages of faith development in his book *Faith After Doubt*. He asks,

> How can parents and faith communities help rising genera-
> tions to grow in faith without getting trapped in small
> boxes? . . . How can we, from the beginning, help people
> keep in mind the ultimate desired end of faith expressing
> itself in love? Obviously, we have to start not with children
> but with ourselves, their parents and teachers. We will re-
> produce what we actually are, not simply what we say or
> wish. It's ridiculous to think that children are like empty
> bowls, and if we pour into them a recipe of Bible stories,
> doctrinal knowledge, songs, lectures, and other religious
> activities, then stir and bake, we will magically help them
> become loving people. Deep personal formation of the next
> generation depends on close-at-hand mentors and models
> who authentically embody the way of life we hope the
> children will "catch" through imitation. The loving hearts of

parents, teachers, and other significant adult models in a child's life are the primary sacred texts from which the child will learn faith expressing itself in love. . . . This is the crisis in religion today: not that children fall short of their parents' faith, but that they grow beyond it. Perhaps, in this light, the much-lamented decline in organized religion is simply a consequence of churches' refusal to stay mindful of the goal of love.

I can trust in my own evolving faith because I have watched my mom outgrow her tiny God as well. The church of her childhood offered a version of God that she would expand. So she helped construct a church around a God who empowered women to lead—not just men. A God who was beautiful, creative, and full of wonder—not stuffy, boring, and stale. A God who was intimate and personal—not distant and generic. A God who drove us to love and serve those in need.

I believe that God is far more loving, expansive, mysterious, complex, wild, ancient, new, and good than we can ever understand or express. May the adults who lead our children continue to transform so that the way we interpret Scripture, treat those who are different, and lead with love reflects the biggest, most gracious, most inclusive version of God we can imagine. Let our churches instill a foundation of faith rooted in love, wonder, justice, and humility. I am grateful to have had that. My expanding vision of God is not impeded by deep wounds. It feels like my soul is stretching rather than repairing. We will almost certainly introduce our children to a small version of God they will outgrow. But let us not introduce them to a God they need to heal from.

3

Monday Through Saturday

Having an External Focus

NANCY

I met my husband one year after he decided to follow Jesus. At just thirty, this tall, dark-haired, lanky guy who loved numbers and games had already found his niche in business. Warren's profession both fascinated and mystified me—he stood all day with his long arms raised high in a pit of shouting commodities traders at the Chicago Board of Trade, most often trading soybeans. After discovering he had an aptitude for this kind of work combined with the luck of tremendous timing in the bull markets of the 1970s, Warren began to make more money than he imagined growing up with his widowed mom and two siblings in the Chicago suburbs.

Warren tells me that on his thirtieth birthday, having already reached some of his financial goals, he experienced a classic moment of melancholy, standing at a mirror and asking himself, *Is this all there is?* At the very same time, by divine "coincidence," Warren's younger brother had come to faith in Christ. Wayne urged his older brother to investigate the claims of Christianity, launching Warren on a year-long quest to explore whether the faith made sense, whether he could be a Christian without checking his brains at the door. Warren is a thinker who lives in his head and is relentlessly curious about everything. Eventually, his exploration through writers like C. S. Lewis and Chuck Colson, along with reading the Bible for the first time in his life, brought Warren to a place of surrender.

God began to do a transforming work on the heart of this young man. Almost immediately Warren discovered a passion for giving, for doing good with what God had entrusted to him. He did a deep dive into any place in Scripture that talked about money and the poor, learning that Jesus talked about both more than anything else. For a brand new Christ-follower, it made perfect sense to Warren that Christians should be abundantly

generous, that those with more would be compelled to give sacri-
ficially, and that global poverty could be eradicated if only all of
us would do our part. As newlyweds we took our first trip to the
developing world, visiting projects in Haiti and Jamaica that we
supported through Compassion International. I was in my early
twenties and had never been exposed to extreme poverty, except
on television. Moments from that first experience are forever
etched in my memory almost forty years later.

One of our visits was to Gonâve Island, an often forgotten
community off the coast of Haiti. There I saw no trees, no flowers,
not even any birds—total desolation. The ground featured
cracked gray mud void of any grass or green, with such harsh
conditions the people could not grow food. Scores of children in
tattered clothes surrounded us, eager to find a way to play soccer
with balled-up pieces of paper. To this day the people of Gonâve
struggle with finding clean water and having reliable electricity.
But the eyes of one woman are what I most remember. Clearly
expecting a baby, she had a couple of other little ones clinging to
her legs. Through a translator I learned that this young mom had
already lost several children to hunger or disease. As she stared
at me, with her hand resting on her protruding belly, she seemed
to be pleading with us that somehow this next child would survive.

Most everyone I know who has visited an area with extreme
poverty or disease returns with a vivid story to tell and was
marked for life by those moments. Warren came back to the
United States determined to play a small part, somehow making
a difference. Much of what I have learned about compassion and
giving people the tools and dignity for work has been a gift from
him. The parable Jesus told in Matthew 25 drives my husband,
who knows that much will be required of those who have been
given much. Eventually, Warren led the global ministry at
Willow Creek for seven years as a full-time volunteer. Because

he didn't grow up in a church, he had no model for traditional missions. This proved to be an advantage, I believe, because Warren applied his strategic thinking to dreaming with his team, always with multiple flipcharts, to figure out how we could develop strategic partnerships with local churches in Africa and Latin America, coming alongside them to assist in the good work that many were already doing. Warren's energy later expanded to local partnerships as well, uncovering opportunities in Chicago to make an impact.

I tell these stories of Warren, knowing that he would be the first to protest and say he should not be elevated as any kind of example, that he was just doing what seemed to be the right thing, that he will be embarrassed by my pride in him. My area of ministry—leading artists to create moments of transcendence in the hour on Sunday—was vastly different from my husband's. And while I believe it matters what takes place when we gather (see chap. 4), I have also come to believe that if churches are going to reach people far from God, we must declare and pursue an external focus.

The watching world wants to know if we are doing anything on the planet to care for the underresourced, to fight for justice and equality, to feed those who are hungry, to visit the prisoner, and to lead the fight against systemic racism. Does the local church have an impact locally and globally?

My friend Mike Breaux tells the story of moving to Southern California, where his daughter is one of the pastors at a local church. Shortly after Mike arrived, he was eating in a restaurant, chatting with a waitress who asked him about his accent (Mike is from Kentucky) and what brought him to town. Mike said they wanted to live near his daughter and son-in-law, and then mentioned the church where they work. The next words from the waitress are what every one of us should long to hear about our community of faith. She said, "Oh, that's the church that does so many good things to help people!" Oh yes, may that be so!

———

At a conference for church leaders where I was invited to teach, I was captivated by a message delivered at that same event by Pastor Ben Cachiaras from Mountain Christian Church in Baltimore. Ben said that serving is the new apologetic. In my years sitting at leadership tables at Willow, we boomers constructed a highly linear process for how we thought most people come to faith. In fact, we described a seven-step process. Now I see that the route many seekers take to Jesus is circuitous, unpredictable, and often messy. Ben described three different big-picture sequences that reveal the approach of churches in the past and then what he sees currently and in the future. It looks like this:

Christ. Community. Cause.

Community. Christ. Cause.

Cause. Community. Christ.

Sequence 1: Christ. Community. Cause. We used to see the most common progression for an individual was first to come to faith, through a relationship and spiritual conversation with a follower of Jesus, combined with front-door accessible experiences at a local church. This approach is now known by many as the attractional model. A conversion then led to community (such as a small group) and then eventually to a person discovering their gifts and beginning to contribute to the cause, making a kingdom impact.

Sequence 2: Community. Christ. Cause. Many faith communities began to see people first exposed to relationships as a response to their longing for community. Some would encounter followers of Christ through an Alpha group or book club or sports team. This might lead to spiritual conversations and then, after coming to faith, the pursuit of the cause was a logical next step, with the new Christ-follower asking, "How can I serve?"

Sequence 3: Cause. Community. Christ. But now Ben suggests that what comes first for many people outside the faith is contributing in some way to help others. Have you noticed how easy it is to recruit a neighbor or coworker to help with a local work project, to serve food at a shelter, to rally around victims of a hurricane or fire or tornado, to stand in a line with a humbling hairnet on their head while packing healthy food for the hungry in the developing world? Most people in our world want to do *something* to make a difference, and they jump at the chance to help in practical ways. Their experience often leads to community, to the beginnings of relationships. And eventually, for some, this will lead to a step of faith and a commitment to Christ. The entire sequence is now often reversed, with serving coming first.

At Soul City Church in Chicago we rally around a firm belief that "church should be seven days a week, not just one!" I believe that every local church, no matter where it is located, should focus on meeting the very real and practical needs of the community around them. This begins with *listening* to discern what those needs are, meeting with local city council members or someone in the mayor's office, asking great questions, uncovering where the biggest hurts lie, and also learning about already-existing organizations that are doing good work and could use the support of a local church with both financial resources and volunteers. In recent years I have been inspired by stories of local churches who have taken these steps and resist the tendency to be insulated in our holy huddles, only caring for the people inside our doors or people in far-away lands.

A tremendous example of external focus comes from the Niagara region of Ontario, Canada. Founded in 1980, this local church with a very long name—Fairview-Louth Mennonite Brethren Community Church—experienced some dynamic numerical growth. The new leadership that grew up in the church was haunted by this question: If our church suddenly disappeared, would anyone in the surrounding society even notice?

What a profound, potentially disturbing, and brave question! They agreed the answer was likely *no*. So they made a bold decision. The church's website says that instead of investing in further expansion at their rural west St. Catharines location, the church moved to within a mile of the downtown core of St. Catharines, seeking to put themselves in greater proximity to people in need. At that point they changed their name to Southridge Community Church to reflect their commitment to serving the community. A year or so after their move, they established a homeless shelter right in their facility. The shelter has fifty-five beds in dorms for men and women. They serve three delicious meals a day and offer personal coaching and recreational programs, spiritual life programming, and sports activities. Since opening in 2005 they have seen more than ten thousand men and women find a place of safety and hope within their church. This shelter is the largest provider of homeless services in the Niagara region.

Not surprisingly, Pastor Jeff Lockyer says this focus on serving has transformed the hearts of those who volunteer. Warren and I had the opportunity to visit the St. Catharines campus, with the shelter just footsteps down the hall from the worship center. Walking into the building on any day of the week reveals love in action. Serving is deeply embedded in their church as the normal, expected activity of every follower of Jesus. The enthusiasm, joy, and commitment to making a real difference were all over the faces of the volunteers we met.

As the church began to expand to become a multisite church, they immediately wondered what each site would focus on for a shelter-equivalent compassion focus. As a result each Southridge location is defined by its unique anchor cause. Their Vineland Community, for example, reaches out to hundreds of Caribbean farm workers who come to the area for seasonal employment. These migrants often deal with loneliness because they are separated from their families during the growing season. The Vineland location is connected with over 250 of these farm workers, providing social events and personal relationships that have spanned several years now.

All of the sites together share a global focus as well, partnering with seven different churches around the world through a partnership with Compassion Canada. And get this—more than *half* of every dollar given to the Southridge churches is invested in local and global outreach! Without a doubt, today the answer to the question whether their church would be missed if it disappeared is a resounding *yes*.

———

As we look at each local church, we can ask whether or not the existence of that church results in

- a decrease in crime?
- plenty of food in the food banks?
- shelter options for people experiencing homelessness?
- visits and intentional relationships at the local jail or prison?
- opportunities for previously incarcerated individuals to get jobs?
- after-school opportunities for young children whose parents are working?
- response to a natural disaster with immediate help?

- medical and dental care for those who cannot afford it?
- legal aid options for the underresourced and immigrants?
- improved, high-quality education opportunities for all children in the area?
- support for people with physical disabilities or mental health challenges?

No church can meet all the needs, but every church can rally around a few causes. During the Covid-19 pandemic, I have found myself celebrating the creative ways many churches have rallied to meet needs. SouthBrook Church in Dayton, Ohio, for example, set up a tent outside the local hospital where volunteer chefs created delicious take-home meals for exhausted health-care workers. Church members also stood in the hospital parking lot, praying for all the patients and medical staff. What a statement it makes to our world when the church is still the church even when we cannot gather on Sunday mornings!

I am not suggesting that we do good and pursue an external focus just so people outside the faith will think well of us. Scripture makes it clear that we should serve and love others primarily because it is the right thing to do, and Jesus commands us to love our neighbors. Just as our Savior came to this planet to serve, so we should mimic his example, bringing hope and practical help to those in great need. As we serve in the name of Christ, the hope is that opportunities will often be stirred up to point people to the good news of the gospel. We are challenged in 1 Peter 3:15 to "always be prepared to answer everyone who asks you to give the reason for the hope that you have." The tension will be to check our motivation and not give out of a place of manipulation or coercion. The church is distinct from a humanitarian organization because we are led by the Spirit and are being transformed by the Spirit. I am struck by how vividly people recall the meeting of a need and can be drawn to the breathtaking goodness of God as a result. But the opposite, sadly, can also be true.

Warren's Aunt Jeanette grew up as the oldest of four children in New York City. Their father died when they were quite young, and the family struggled to meet basic needs. Aunt Jeanette was supposed to pay a fee for the confirmation class at their local church. The family didn't have the funds. Aunt Jeanette remembers the shame of that experience as the church leaders put on pressure for them to pay or she would not be included in the class. Meanwhile, a Jewish rabbi lived nearby. He became aware of Jeanette and the challenges of her family and began helping them with food and clothing. Aunt Jeanette was so deeply marked by the contrast of those two faith communities that later in life she married a Jewish man and converted.

It's so easy for our local churches to become so consumed with building our own ministries inside the church that we lose sight of our calling to be a radiant light in the darkness. As we seek to steward our limited resources—and every church has limited resources—I challenge us to assess where we are investing dollars and time. How much is tilted toward more ingrown ministries and how much is generously offering hope to the local and global community? A quote commonly attributed to Saint Francis of Assisi sums it up better than I can: "Preach the gospel at all times and when necessary use words."

SAMANTHA

"What institution was intended to be a place where anyone could go to have their needs met?" My senior English class was stumped. In the third-story corner classroom of our large public high school, we were discussing some texts meant to help us consider the elements of intentional communities or utopian villages. Mr. Sanders was a patient teacher. He let us bat around ideas ("A hospital?"), gently prompting us to think deeper (*"all* needs—physical, mental, emotional"). "A courthouse?" someone offered. "A place where *anyone* could go, not just those who could afford it," he guided us back to the question, like bumper rails for our bowling balls of ideas. We were fast, if not accurate.

Eventually, silence fell. There was nowhere *anyone* could go to have *all* their needs met!

Mr. Sanders rarely offered answers, but it seemed we were never going to arrive at this possibility without assistance.

"The local church," he said.

We looked at him, blankly. He suggested that at one time the local church was seen as a place where the hurting could be connected to resources in the community—whether they needed food, grief support, a bed, or legal aid. The church could serve as a central hub connecting those in need to ministries, partners, or contributions from those in excess (or whatever you call the opposite of "in need").

The very idea—that in a healthy society the church might fill an essential role of need-meeting like no other institution could—was deeply compelling. So much so that it's one of the only classroom moments I remember from all of high school.

I never had much luck getting any of my friends in the Chicago theater scene to visit my church on a Sunday—not even on Easter or Christmas. But one weekend our church canceled services to go out and serve the city. I signed up to help sort clothes in a homeless shelter. When my group leader texted us that we could use a few more volunteers, I sent out a text early Sunday morning to eight friends—folks who had never been to or participated in Soul City Church before. Within an hour all eight showed up at the homeless shelter. It was the easiest invitation I ever made. And apparently— even for my friends who were skeptical about showing up at church—showing up to a homeless shelter was a very easy yes.

We are a socially conscious generation, passionate and eager to rally around efforts to combat injustice. Growing up with the internet has meant growing up exposed to inequality. This witnessing has formed us. We want to be part of restoration. I believe that if the church were to place a disproportionate emphasis on responsive and sustained service to the vulnerable, young people would flock to be a part of it.

The very first words of Jesus' public ministry cast a vision of abundant liberation and generosity:

The Spirit of the Lord is on me,
because he has anointed me
to proclaim good news to the poor.
He has sent me to proclaim freedom for the prisoners
and recovery of sight for the blind,
to set the oppressed free,
to proclaim the year of the Lord's favor. (Luke 4:16-19)

What if this mission were front and center in our faith communities?

I think it would bring people like Sarah Grace back to church. Though she was introduced to faith at a young age, like many of my friends, Sarah Grace has been on a journey away from the church, disillusioned by "unhumble" pastors, silence in the face of injustice, and exclusionary thinking. But in the years since she stopped feeling at home in church as she knew it, her spirituality has continued to deepen and she now finds herself longing to be part of a community again. So, she's been poking around websites.

"I just want to be a part of the church that's doing the *most* good. If I saw a website with a mission statement that said, 'We don't claim to know everything, but what we are trying to do is make positive change for these groups of people who've been left behind, and here are all the places that we invest our resources of time and money,' well, that's where I would go." At that point she stopped herself and asked an important question: "Although, I guess, why wouldn't I just go join a volunteer organization? What's the difference?"

Alison's lifelong journey with missions began with her conversion. At a Christian concert she prayed the sinner's prayer, and the next summer she convinced her parents to go on a mission trip to Monterey, Mexico. "We knocked on doors and read a script," she remembers, "We said, 'Hi, do you have a moment? You have sin in your heart.' The word for *sin* in Spanish is one letter different from *fish*. It was very easily mistaken for 'you have fish in your heart,'" she laughs. At their debriefings, "it was always a number. How many lives got saved? Something about it didn't sit right." But in other ways, this trip was deeply formative. Her first exposure to extreme poverty led her to make a lifelong commitment to serving those in need.

The American approach to missions continues to evolve. Writing for the *Atlantic* in her 2018 article "A New Generation Redefines What It Means to Be a Missionary," Saba Imtiaz remarks,

The profile of a typical Christian missionary is changing—and so is the definition of their mission work, which historically tended to center on the explicit goal of converting people to Christianity. While some denominations, particularly evangelicalism, continue to emphasize this, Christian missionaries nowadays are relatively less inclined to tell others about their faith by handing out translated Bibles, and more likely to show it through their work—often a tangible social project, for example in the context of a humanitarian crisis.

I wonder whether our hearts and minds are transforming alongside our methods. While one can certainly point to evidence of life change and sacrifice in the work of the overseas American missionaries supported by their local churches over the past fifty years, Alison's experience also indicates a culturally irresponsible approach to service. And of course these people and the strategies they employed were products of their time, just as I am confined to mine. Yet I can't help but notice the ties between that model of missions and how the White American church has historically wedded evangelism to conquest and assimilation. Through the prophetic leadership of writers such as Lisa Sharon Harper, Kaitlin Curtice, and Jemar Tisby, I am beginning to see these layers in our missional work and in my own heart. And even as our strategies evolve, I need the church to disciple me in this unlearning.

The work of detangling the white-savior complex from our approach to serving demands our careful and humble attention. If our service elevates our status, prioritizes our culture, preserves our comfort, and saves souls but ignores bodies, we are bringing the gospel of *us*, not the gospel of Jesus.

I am humbled by how deeply embedded this framework is. Recently our church was discussing Christmas service opportunities, and we were about to move forward on plans to provide turkey dinners for the residents of a nearby government housing community we often partner with. I thought it was a great idea and was about to solve the refrigeration challenge of storing ninety-seven turkeys when someone spoke up and said, "Is this what those families really want?"

It took all of about thirty seconds to realize that this community, primarily made up of Mexican immigrants, probably would not choose turkey, mashed potatoes, and cranberry sauce if they could afford a nice Christmas dinner. But critical thinking shouldn't *stop* us from engaging with those who are suffering. The fear of getting it wrong can be paralyzing. The desire to do good *well* must lead us to slow down long enough to listen and move forward thoughtfully.

Our team pursued further conversation with a leader from the community to land on a way to serve that would yield back some agency and dignity to the recipients. There can be great teaching moments for our congregation if we possess the humility and presence to name the troubling remnants of our past when they surface—if we focus on not just serving the poor but *how*.

For twenty-five years Ron Bueno has served as the executive director of ENLACE, a nonprofit that equips local churches in El Salvador, Nepal, Guatemala, and the United States to transform their communities. He has spent decades brokering partnerships between US churches and churches in the emerging world. In his work relating to the US church staff members appointed to lead compassion and justice projects, Ron has observed the expectation placed on them: to prioritize engaging as many church members as possible in service opportunities. "Their mandate is not impact, their mandate is mobilization," he notes.

For most churches you go into a community, you identify the need, you provide based on what you can do, and basically the person in the community is passive and receptive at every stage of your outreach. What you're telling them is, "I know better than you what you need. I'm gonna give out of my surplus. I'm not concerned about you creating the ability to change your situation yourself." Because the value of community change or impact is entirely missing from our outreach. That's not prioritized. It's not valued within your church's mission strategy. Leaders want to know how many people showed up on Serve Day and how many people did they serve.

Ron recognizes that mobilization matters to pastors because discipleship matters. *Of course.* Serving transforms us. Exposure to poverty changes us.

How would we approach missions differently if *impact* and sustainable, community-led change became a greater priority? What if it became *the* priority? Would the goal of discipleship necessarily suffer?

I wonder.

Every March we knew it was coming. We binged on chocolate in the days leading up. We whined. We cheated with Chipotle. With great detail, we planned out our first "real" meal back. When it came time for Rice and Beans Week, we behaved like children. Because we were.

As preteens my sister and I were not great sports when it came to this portion of Willow's annual month-long awareness-raising and fundraising efforts to support communities experiencing hunger and a lack of clean water. Every year our upper-middle-class church was challenged to eat only rice and beans for one week. It was an exercise intended to increase our empathy for and attention to the massive part of the world that lives on this diet every day. We were also invited to constrict our serving size of

rice and beans to experience—in a fractional, momentary way—
what it would be like to go to bed hungry.

I was about twelve years old the first year our church issued this
challenge. I had not yet traveled to far-reaching corners of the globe
marked by extreme poverty. While I had an attitude about this idea
("You know this isn't even actually *doing* anything, right Dad? People
are still starving whether I pretend to or not"), over the years it was
deeply formative. At school I had to explain to friends why my lunch
looked the way it did. This prompted middle school discussions
about injustice, how easy it is to ignore the realities of poverty in our
suburban bubble, and how that was, like, pretty cool that we talked
about that stuff at church. And at our family dinners we couldn't
ignore the reality of global hunger because it was staring at us from
our plate. I still remember one night when Mom was deciding who
to give the last scoop of rice and beans—me because I had a bas
ketball game or Dad because he'd had a hard work day—and she was
moved, thinking of moms who face those excruciating decisions daily.

I can finally admit I was wrong (sometimes it takes twenty
years). Rice and Beans Week *was* doing something. In me and in
my family. Discipleship was happening, and when the invitation
came at church to make a financial contribution to provide clean
water to families we would never meet, whose names we would
never know, it was an easy yes. And we didn't have to take a plane
to Africa to find passion in our hearts. We didn't waste any of our
partner organizations' precious time on mobilization.

After living in Mexico for several years as a missionary (and
newlywed), Alison and her husband, Jason, moved to Chicago.
Alison longed to experience a more expansive definition of
mission. *Could we be the hands and feet of Jesus without telling
people they're wrong?* she wondered.

That's when she discovered Safe Families, a local organization
designed to bring stability to families in distress. "You become an

extended family for those on the margins who don't have somewhere safe to turn." This included taking in young kids for short-term care to support moms in need. "We hosted a mom who was fifteen years old," she remembers. "Her dad had sold her into sex trafficking." Alison worked with several women, providing mentorship, care, and love. She quickly moved from being a host home to becoming a family coach.

When she moved to Texas, Alison tried to launch Safe Families in Houston. She tried again when she came to Austin. In both cities she was involved in large, resourced churches where she thought there would be a natural groundswell of support for this kind of partnership.

"I found a lot of resistance to working with the mom," she recounts, sadly. "People are very scared. They wanted the cute baby, but they didn't want to open their homes to the moms."

I wish I didn't see myself in this. I would like to do good *and* feel good. I would like to do good on my schedule. I would like to do good without sacrifice. I would like to look good while doing good. I would like to change someone's life in one hour or twenty-five dollars a month. I would like it if afterward someone could show me what I fixed. I would like to imagine myself a fixer.

We need this discipleship piece to serve as Jesus modeled—with a posture of humility, patience, and respect. This doesn't come naturally (at least not to me). When churches integrate weekend programming and education alongside service opportunities, we might become more thoughtful servants with braver hearts. I think this is the answer to Sarah Grace's very good question. A missional church understands that our inner work is inextricably linked with our outer work: that we must transform ourselves to transform the world.

When Will and I moved to Austin for his graduate school program, we found our way to Austin New Church for one reason:

we saw on social media that instead of an Easter service, they grilled hamburgers for the homeless. This sounded like a church community that my justice-driven husband might feel at home in and that my megachurched-high-production-value self might need to recover in. (*I thought you did twelve services on Easter, not zero!*)

Alison had just become the mission director at Austin New Church. Around this time the immigrant families being separated and held in detainment at the border were getting more attention in the media. At the urging of our bishop, Alison determined to make this a primary focus of our church's missional work.

But she would build on her experience. She wouldn't risk misguided conversations about the fish in anyone's heart. Alison set up a church trip to the border and invited only Spanish-speakers to join. "I didn't want people going to gawk, to look at them [the immigrants] like they're animals." This team came back and shared about the experience, which had deeply affected them, and those ripples reverberated throughout the congregation. They also returned with prayer cards from kids inside one of the camps, letting the kids know a congregation was praying for them and asking what we could pray for specifically. Alison incorporated these prayers into Sunday services. And the heartbreaking, haunting words of children in an unspeakable situation began to shift something in my heart and the hearts of our community.

Alison also found local partners who were already providing support to immigrants and asylum seekers. She formed relationships with leaders and learned what the needs were. There were some concrete ways we could plug in: driving families to appointments and helping kids with homework. Above all, these folks were desperately lonely. Surely, this was a need the church could help meet.

Alison knew from her Safe Families disappointment that this relationship piece wouldn't be simple. She put together a series of workshops for folks interested in volunteering. I attended, curious but worried that I had nothing to offer. All that remained of my high school Spanish was breakfast food. The workshops prepared us for the discomfort of being with someone who doesn't speak our language. Trauma-informed social workers taught us what questions to steer clear of and how to respect and protect the difficult parts of someone's story. An immigrant from Guatemala shared her journey and how several key friendships had helped her tremendously in adjusting to life in Austin.

Of course, nothing can fully prepare someone for a woman from the Congo sitting in the front seat of their car, her precious baby in the back. But our ministry had prepared me to *expect* discomfort. And maybe that at least motivates you to endure it.

We drove to Walmart. In addition to her native African language, she spoke French, Portuguese, and had picked up Spanish on her journey by foot through Mexico and across our border. She humored me as I called out various vocabulary words as they occurred to me, adding a question mark to see if any might be on her shopping list. "Huevos? Jamón? Avena?"

Why is this girl obsessed with breakfast? she must have wondered. *How many of these trips until we are friends?* I wondered.

She needed clothing. After picking out some business attire, we made our way to the checkout, and she saw something that caught her attention: a tank top hanging near the front. A weather word popped into my head from the recesses of a dusty Spanish attic in the back of my brain. I shook off the cobwebs and tried it.

"Calor?"

"Sí," she smiled, ever gracious. A tank top for the heat.

As she placed the tank on the conveyor belt, she pointed at the words, and I noticed the text splashed across the shirt for the first time. She wanted to know what they meant.

Far beyond my translation capabilities, I simply spoke the words aloud in English, "The struggle is real."

These words—a derivative of hip-hop culture used to depict the hardships of systemic racism—have now become something else. Some kind of a cultural motto for people my age who are asked to "adult" or get up before 8:00 a.m. or send an actual package at the actual post office.

And, Vandi—a woman 7,743 miles away from her home, escaping who-knows-what terror, who walked through entire countries to get to this country, with a baby on her back—repeated the words after me in English, not yet understanding them (though with her multilingual mind, it would surely only be a matter of time). "The struggle is real."

I gave her nothing more than a ride to and from Walmart, but simple proximity to her resilience and strength showed me the face of Jesus that day. It reminded me how cavalier I have come to be about certain "struggles" in my own life. Watching her care for her child, I thought of the literal oceans she had crossed to provide her baby with a better life. Her tenacity, the ferociousness of her love, marked me. It taught me about the nature of God's love for us. Relationships with those who are suffering *is* discipleship. Alison says, "We have so much to learn from these people! I don't think Americans realize . . ."

She is still frustrated by the church's hesitancy to pursue these relationships. She won't yet call the partnership between Austin New Church and Posada Esperanza (House of Hope) a success story. I can't say that Vandi is my friend yet. I don't visit as regularly as I meant to. As I write this, we are all cloistered in our "pods" due to Covid-19. I am wondering how to provide aid to those most affected by this disease. There are so many in need.

But perhaps we have to tamper our love affair with mission "success stories." With big serve-day turnouts and the number of buildings built. When I asked Ron what is the number one thing he wishes churches knew about partnering with nonprofits who aid those in need, he answered without missing a beat, "I wish churches understood the enormity of the cause." He says, "I would like the US church to realize the complexity of poverty, how structural, how broken, how endemic these issues are. It's not a one-off. It's not an exchange. It can't happen quickly. We've got to invest over a long period of time and be patient."

That will require us to cultivate in ourselves and our congregations an appetite for sustainable impact rather than a doing-good dopamine hit. To unpack the layers of privilege and history that led to this most ultimate irony of a Congolese asylum-seeker walking around Austin in a Walmart shirt that reads "The struggle is real."

It's harder work than I thought. But, oh, wouldn't it be worth the discomfort, the difficult conversations, the rerouting, the undoing, the lament, and the patience if the church could become known as a place where needs are met? Such that a senior English class would immediately think of it and get on with their lesson.

4

You Had to Be There

Concerning the Hour on Sunday

NANCY

We stood six feet apart in our church's parking lot on a warm August Sunday morning. This was the first gathering of Soul City Church since March 2020 when the global pandemic swept through our land and overturned everything we assumed was normal about coming together. Seven months of digital connection. And then an email invitation to make a reservation, only if healthy, wear a mask, and come together to focus primarily on prayer for our city and our world. Maybe one hundred of us showed up, tentatively taking a spot marked with duct tape on the ground, with half our faces hidden. But we could see one another's eyes—the windows to the soul.

I met my younger daughter, Johanna, and chose a spot near her and a few of her small-group twenty-something friends. All summer our city and world had been facing not only the ruthless virus but also a racial reckoning marked by protest and in some cases violence in our city. So I was looking into the eyes of friends and other attenders, seeing some fear, anxiety, excitement, weariness, loneliness, hope, and despair. A worship leader began to strum a familiar song, and we attempted to sing a little through our masks. That's when I became undone for the first time that morning. How long it had been since any of us worshiped in the presence of others—unless our roommates or family joined us in a living room! I tried to choke out the song with a lump in my throat and tears in my eyes, recognizing my deep hunger and thirst for once again being among the family of God.

I treasured several profound moments in that brief one-hour experience, including the moment when we raised our hands to pray over our troubled city, the city we love. Our arms are all different colors. We represent the incredible diversity of Chicago, and together we called out to God our lament for the divisiveness in our world, for all that is broken, begging for healing and unity. I felt like a hot mess between the moisture from the mask and tears leaking from my eyes. But it was a beautiful hot mess. Afterward, Johanna and I lingered for a while. No one seemed to want to leave quickly. Eventually, we found our way to our pastors and friends, Jarrett and Jeanne Stevens. They shared their own emotions on that day, and we kept saying, "It's just so good to be together."

As I write, our church is beginning to gather in our indoor space with masks and reservations. Some people speculate about whether church services will ever get back to anything we recognize as normal. It's hard for me to imagine standing shoulder to shoulder in our community, chairs butted up against one another, singing freely, holding up arms when we want to, hugging friends when it's over, breathing the same air for seventy minutes, and feeling anything like safe.

By the time this book is printed, I'm assuming there will be some progress in the gathering experience. Meanwhile, church leaders are wondering, *Is the gathering, the corporate experience, dead? Is it even necessary?* or at the very least, *How will it be different going forward?* Church attenders have become accustomed to streaming their church service in pajamas or sweatpants, over breakfast with the newspaper or phone, either live or whenever they decide to replay the podcast later. It's been comfortable and easy, playing into the worst of our consumer tendencies. If we're completely honest, we may have television on in the background. It's so relaxed! Some may never want to get in their car or take public transportation back to regular gatherings.

———

While I have no crystal ball to forecast the future, I do believe that the gathering as we know it will die *if* it's only about the delivery of content. Now that all of us can listen to a message from any pastor around the world on our little screens or even worship with a team of our choosing even if they are far, far away, why would we be motivated to physically show up at a specific time and place if only to hear a message and maybe sing a few songs? I don't believe content will drive anyone to make the effort. There must be far more to the experience that would cause a person to say, "You had to be there!"

Back in 2004, which honestly feels like a hundred years ago to me, I released a book titled *The Hour on Sunday: Creating Moments of Transformation and Wonder*. The book captured my passion for what can happen when we come together on a Sunday morning. I currently use a stack of four of the unsold books that linger in my office to raise my computer for Zoom calls so I look better (according to the advice of Zoom experts anyway). But until recently I hadn't read my book for a long time. As I skimmed through the chapters, this sentence leaped out at me: "I have never believed more strongly in the potential of the hour on Sunday."

Interesting. Do I still believe that now? How invested am I in caring about what happens or doesn't happen when a church opens its doors on Sunday morning or whenever that community chooses to gather? As I sit with these questions, the big-picture answer I offer is *yes*. I believe even more strongly in the potential of the hour on Sunday! But the key word is, of course, *potential*.

Why should we invest resources and time creating experiences on Sunday mornings if followers of Jesus can do all these same things at home, individually, whenever and however they choose? For it's true that we can always

- pray alone.
- worship alone.
- confess and lament alone.
- be silent alone.
- receive teaching alone.
- take the sacrament alone.

To be clear, I believe we can and should frequently engage these spiritual practices in solitude. But something profoundly different happens when we practice them together. When the followers of Jesus gather in a space of any kind to offer praise to God, to sit in silence or lament, to confess our sins through guided prayers, to hear the Word of God taught and learn as one, to celebrate and remember our Savior at the Table with the bread and the cup, to lift up individuals and our communities in prayer, and even to laugh at the absurdities of our humanness—all of these are opportunities for moments of wonder and transcendence.

That's why the words *together* and *one another* abound in the pages of Scripture. God is magnified when we are together, and often we learn from one another how to follow him with greater intimacy and devotion throughout the rest of our week. As a teen if I pushed back about "going to church," my parents would quote Hebrews 10:24-25: "Let us . . . not give up meeting together, as some are in the habit of doing, but encouraging one another."

For over fifty years now, I have both attended and helped to create countless hours on Sunday in more than one local church. What do I see now as I look in the rearview mirror? What do I believe is still true and needs to be held on to, and what is essential to reinvent for the future? One of my observations is that church leaders and key volunteers tend to swing pendulums. We often look at values or strategies as all-or-nothing rather than as tensions to be delicately managed. Maybe it's just easier to overreact and push ourselves into the land of extremes. I'd like to explore five of these tensions, these pendulum swings, to discern what will be helpful for the future of church gatherings and those who plan them.

Attractional versus missional. Back in the 1970s, 1980s, and beyond, I played a central role in designing what became known as *seeker services*. Those of us who helped to found Willow Creek were passionately motivated to create a church experience for people outside the family of God, for our friends who had no interest in church and considered it to be boring and irrelevant to their daily lives. So we set aside our own traditions and preferences, started with a blank sheet of paper, and asked hard questions about what we could create for our friends. We thought through the entire experience they would have from the moment they arrived at the movie theater to the moment they left.

This entire design was based on a two-pronged strategy. At the same time we poured ourselves into creating seeker services, we also designed a midweek experience on Wednesday nights for the believer. Almost all of our devoted Christ-followers committed to participating in *both* of these gatherings. Wednesday nights we worshiped unapologetically and then studied God's Word in much greater depth than what was offered on Sundays. Very few churches have been able to sustain a commitment to this kind of two-pronged strategy.

What we created for the weekends is now referred to as *attractional* ministry. The basic idea focuses on what we can design that will give Christ-followers an easy invitation to their friends from work or in the neighborhood. This strategy assumes that the believing core of your church will intentionally build relationships with others and then discern with the Spirit's guidance when it might be time to invite someone to church. The believer would have confidence that on any given Sunday their friend would feel welcome and not threatened, that the experience would offer an introduction to Christianity, that there would be moments in the hour when the arts or the teaching would potentially move them a step closer to God and his love for them. We often referred to Sunday mornings as the front door for seekers as they explored the faith.

Many churches around the globe began to create similar kinds of weekend gatherings. And there were thousands of people who eventually came to faith through these efforts. How many of those seeds have taken root is a matter of much debate. An alternative movement to attractional ministry emerged, moving away from a strong emphasis on Sunday morning—this is called the *missional* approach. A missional church has been defined as having a "posture toward the world." It is a community organized around being an agent of God's mission to the world. As I described in chapter three, the local church must be defined by and known for the difference they make in their community—for what happens seven days a week, not just one.

The tension between attractional and missional, in my view, is not necessary. For some individuals a Sunday gathering will not be the front door—and for others it might. What if we stopped looking at this as a kind of competition and choose instead to embrace and celebrate the massive potential of our God to reach people with a boundless list of options? A healthy church opens its doors throughout the week and also gets outside of those doors to serve and reach people right where they are.

Performance versus participation. One of the most hurtful criticisms lobbed at seeker services is that it's all about the show or performance. In the past decade I observed many churches that avoid any element that could seem *performed*. The new value is full participation in every aspect of worship except for listening to the teaching. In fact, the very word *worship* has become a synonym for singing. We invite people to stand for *worship*, and we all sing everything together. No one sings a solo or presents a song as a moment (unless it's part of teaching us all a new song). We have also seen a narrowing use of the arts to essentially music and video in most of our churches. Art forms such as spoken word, poetry, drama, dance, or even instrumental music have largely been relegated to a rare holiday service if used at all. Underneath these changes is a fundamental belief that if I'm watching something, I'm not worshiping.

I suggest that this assumption should be revisited and challenged. Worship is so much more than singing. Artists who share their gifts in church open up windows to our soul, and God often moves us deeply as we experience moments together. We can be invited into the transcendent by witnessing, hearing, seeing, touching, not only by singing. This leads me to the next tension.

Authenticity versus excellence. In *An Hour on Sunday*, I wrote, "If I had to choose just one supreme value, I'd pick authenticity over excellence and creativity simply because the door to attenders' hearts and minds will slam shut the instant they pick up on pretense of any kind." I stand by those words today. But somewhere along the way many church folks have decided that the values of authenticity and excellence cannot coexist. Excellence is *doing the best you can with what you have*, which honors God. And beauty points the way to our Creator. Of course, excellence implies planning and practice. We don't become excellent at anything overnight. (The professional golfer Gary Player is known for his declaration that "The more I practice, the luckier I get!") Excellence is not the same thing as neurotic perfectionism. It's all about giving every endeavor intentional focus and hard work, to make something beautiful and good.

Why is it that when we see something happen in church that seems to be totally spontaneous or even sloppy or mediocre, we tend to attribute greater authenticity to that moment than when something is executed with care and beauty? As I have long pondered this question, I think perhaps we have come to believe that the Holy Spirit only works right at the moment, that something is more real if it was *not* planned. And of course we also like to see things that are not perfect because it reminds us of our common humanity and limits. One more quote from my previous book captures my view on planning versus spontaneity:

Don't assume that service elements planned a month in advance are somehow less spiritual than moments that occur spontaneously. Our God is as fully capable of flowing his power to artists and teachers a few weeks in advance as he is able to do so in the moment. It's mistaken to believe that planning automatically gets in the way of what God might want to do.

Every person who plays a part in creating church gatherings will need to manage this tension of authenticity and excellence. If we guard our hearts and see ourselves accurately, we will be the real deal. We can be transparent, vulnerable, truthful, humble, and excellent at the same time!

Unpredictable versus template. When you attend your church's weekend gathering, do you know what is going to happen, in what order, on most Sundays? If I asked you to write down the typical order of service, could you do it with ease? Whether your church is more traditional or contemporary, I think most of us have a form of liturgy, a template. Church teams usually employ an online tool to keep track of the services they are designing and to communicate to volunteers what is coming up. These online tools offer a template approach so that worship leaders can plug in elements as they are selected.

I believe there is another approach to consider that allows for greater freedom and the possibility of surprise. What if we shake things up and start the gathering in a whole new way? What if we unleash the arts to prepare people for the teaching or even weave artistic elements throughout the sermon? What if people were motivated to show up on time because they don't want to miss anything and aren't sure how the worship service will begin?

There are solid arguments to suggest that a predictable template brings a sense of comfort and confidence to your core attenders, especially if they choose to bring a friend. I am a devoted viewer of the *Today Show* in the morning. I can tell you with great accuracy what time the news, weather, "Morning Boost," and "Pop Start" will be every day. If the producers of that show decided to mess with their template, it would throw me off!

So what is the right answer? I don't think there is one. We can be creative within a template approach if we choose to ask how an element can be done in a fresh way. But I also believe that on occasion it is wise to cause people to sit on the edge of their seats, not knowing what is going to happen next, surprised by a moment they did not see coming. My concern with templates and online planning tools is that if we are not careful, they can permit us to get lazy. Those tools are great for communication, but they do not replace the need for brainstorming, for the hard work of asking how we can design an experience each week with the potential to move people and offer a moment of wonder.

Topical teaching versus biblical exegesis. Another big swing of the pendulum concerns the teaching or preaching time in the weekly gathering. Pastors began to teach in series, focusing on felt needs and topics that offer an easy invitation to bring new people on board. Great attention is paid at many churches to titles, graphics, and the branding of these series. On average, a series might last three to six weeks.

But then concern arose about messages that seemed to be only lightly rooted in Scripture, using just a verse or two to support the theme of the day but not digging into the Bible with any depth. As some leaders sought to discern the level of true transformation among their regular attenders, they became alarmed at the abysmal level of biblical illiteracy. Responding to a wave of requests for Sunday mornings to be deeper, some teachers swung the pendulum to another extreme—teaching a book of the Bible verse by verse, slowly, using all the tools of biblical exegesis, even if it meant a church spent half a year or

more in one book. Some of these teachers still offered applications
—how does this matter in your everyday life?—while others just
seemed to want to fill the heads of their people with more and
more knowledge and information, assuming the listener could
figure out later how to apply it.

There is no one right way to do church and certainly not one
right answer about teaching. In recent years I have attended
churches where the teaching is twenty minutes or less, with one
big idea, and churches with forty-five-minute sermons. Of course
in many communities the teaching diet is determined by the
church calendar and Scriptures outlined for each week.

My main concern, no matter the length or style of the messages, is that our ultimate goal is to have a clear answer to the
question, So what? Church is not fundamentally a classroom
where we seek to fill our minds with abundant information. The
question that must drive all of us as teachers of the Word is, If the
listener applies this teaching, if the Holy Spirit does what only
the Spirit can do, how will life be different throughout the coming
week, and in what ways will the listener become more like Jesus?
The stated mission of my church, Soul City, is this: "To lead people
into a transforming relationship with Jesus." That is what the
goal of any gathering, including the teaching, needs to be.

I am not a fan of church shopping and have always urged Christ-
followers to commit themselves for the long haul to a local church,
even when it becomes apparent that no church is perfect. So after
over thirty years of investment in the Willow community, deciding it was time to leave was excruciating for Warren and me.
Would we look for a similar kind of church? Could I possibly set
aside my tendency to critique the Sunday gathering and enter
into the experience with an open mind and heart?

A beloved friend and spiritual director offered me some much-needed wisdom. She suggested that maybe, if only for a short season, Warren and I might consider becoming part of a church very different from what we had known before, seeking a season of new perspective and healing. Eventually, we found ourselves driving an hour to another sleepy suburb and an Episcopal church. Neither of us was at all familiar with a liturgical style of service. Let me describe our first Sunday at St. Mark's.

We drove up to a beautiful stone building, parked our car (close to the entrance!), and tentatively walked into the lobby area. We must have looked new because shortly after arriving, a man in a robe sporting a warm smile introduced himself. Turns out he was Pastor Mark, though not the saint the church is named for. He asked for our names, which we gave to him. Just before going in to take our seats, I did something I never do—I signed a book in the lobby for visitors and even gave our home address.

The next hour could not have been more different from our usual experience on Sunday mornings. We tried to follow along with standing, sitting, or even kneeling on the little benches below our pew. We spoke beautiful prayers and were led in a time of confession. My only complaint was that the time of silence to confess our sins was way too brief for my list!

A small choir sounded bigger than it was because of the wonderful acoustics. Then Pastor Mark came to the floor in front and delivered a well-thought-out twenty-minute message based on the Scriptures for the day. My husband, with his limited attention span, loved the shorter message. Everything in the service built up to the Sacrament. Row by row we were guided to the front for the bread and the cup. We took turns kneeling. Pastor Mark made his way to us, and as he gave us the Communion elements, I was stunned to hear him say, "Warren, this is the body of Christ.

Nancy, this is the body of Christ." We had only met him a short hour before, and he had remembered our names!

Warren and I found a little place for brunch and a debrief on our experience. I was surprised that he felt drawn in and wanted to return. After a beautiful drive home on some country roads, we pulled into our driveway and saw a basket by the front door. Nestled in the basket were a fresh loaf of bread, a little silver cross, and a note that simply said, "Thank you for joining us at St. Mark's today!" How did this basket magically appear? We found out the following Sunday that Mark and his wife like to look at the book in the lobby and deliver a basket to each visitor who dared to share an address. They had to drive an hour to our home and did it with joy!

Our experience at St. Mark's reminded me of the power of personal connection, of sacraments in the context of community, of the wonder of feeling seen and valued. We made that church our community for about eighteen months before sensing a leading to use our gifts at Soul City Church. I will be forever grateful for the ways God used St. Mark's to help us heal and to experience the hour on Sunday in fresh ways that fed our souls.

━━━

I have experienced church gatherings in widely different places around the globe—everything from a repurposed bowling alley in New Jersey to a glorious cathedral in London to a small hut with a grass roof in Zimbabwe. I hold tightly to the vision that what we experience together has the potential to shape, move, and transform us. And while a thriving church is about all seven days of the week, the catalyst for life change and ministry impact is often propelled by what God will do among us next Sunday! Therefore I declare, *The hour on Sunday isn't everything . . . but it can truly be something!*

SAMANTHA

Why isn't church more beautiful? Whenever I hear my mom trace the map of her life, this question grabs me. It's what she remembers wondering as a young girl, trying to sit quietly through stuffy church services. This question became her compass. The arts ministry she went on to build included actors, dancers, designers, painters, and storytellers. Because of them I grew up sitting in church wondering, *How can I be a part of this?* Not just this community and these performances—although, to be clear, I once *lived for* being cast in a "big church" drama sketch—but I was also compelled to be part of this family of believers, enticed by an ancient story that wasn't over yet. On Sundays my imagination soared. It was in church that I discovered my love for theater and my gift for writing. It was in church that I first witnessed the power of the arts to disrupt, comfort, name, provoke, question, and transform.

It wasn't until I left for college and set out into the awkward church-going years in between youth group and parenting that I realized that not every church staff had a drama director! I felt disillusioned. Born into a community where the arts were fully unleashed and integrated, it was like they had all been stuffed back in the box. I sensed the untapped creativity of each community I was part of lying dormant, under the predictability and relaxed energy of the young churches I sought out. Sometimes I thought of the full-scale original church musicals I got to be a part of in middle school, of the drama scenes that made me laugh until I peed, of the dancers who made my spirit soar one Easter morning. People cringed when I tried to describe these things. I learned church drama had a terrible reputation. I started to question my memories and taste. It felt like waking up from a dream and into a ministry world without room for me.

So, I turned elsewhere with my creative gifts. I spent the last decade pursuing a career in theater, where I got to work with other people who believed deeply in the power of transcendent moments. I would spend hours rehearsing one beat of one scene, working with collaborators to see how we could shift the temperature of the room with the right pause. I learned how important the beginning of a gathering is, spending the first three hours of tech week on the moment before the first words are spoken. Lights, then music. *No*, music, then lights.

I sat at the feet of gifted directors who create immersive theatrical experiences. I watched how they took care of an unsure audience when introducing a new way to participate. Time and again I saw audience members delight at a well-structured opportunity to connect with a stranger. I experienced a production of *Our Town* that was different from every other production I've seen because the seats were arranged in such a way that the audience could see one another. So when the character Emily looks back on her life and says, "Oh, it goes by so fast!" I saw over the actress's shoulder as a single tear fell down the face of an older woman in the audience. I will never forget that moment, how it gripped my soul and begged me to remember the preciousness of my only life, all because someone thought, *What if we didn't put the seats in rows? What then?*

Every so often a church would nip at my heels like a lousy ex-boyfriend who only texts when he misses you: Christmas. Churches started inviting me to help craft creative elements for their Christmas services. The stakes always felt high. Without taking artistic risks the rest of the year, would the congregation be prepared for this interruption? How could I create something that would fit within their culture? How do I avoid anything cringey? What makes someone cringe?

I sensed that something had shifted. My friends have no patience for rock-concert lighting. They don't want a church that feels too slick, branded, or aggressively hip. They wonder why money was spent on elaborate sets, fancy videos, and bigger auditoriums. And if the stage rises up and out of the floor, they will have a hard time listening to anything that comes next.

I suppose we are always building in reaction to what we inherited. The productions my mom's team created were undeniably powerful, drawing large crowds and changing widely held perceptions about what church is: namely, I think, they helped to change a generation's understanding that church was irrelevant and boring. But with my peers I sensed a new barrier to entry. It is an impression forged by a reputation defined by what (and who) we are against: massive political power, an allegiance to white supremacy, a disregard for science, and other reasons we'll explore further in chapter six. For some it is a suspicion shaped by their church's rigid focus on correct beliefs absent of the feeling of embodied love. My friends don't worry that church is boring. They worry that the institution can't be trusted.

Perhaps sensing this seed of suspicion, the look and feel of Sunday gatherings are evolving in certain places. Some churches have moved toward a service that feels wholly unproduced and laid-back. The farm-to-table approach wants you to know it has nothing to hide. No matter how long the meal takes, you can trust that it's all prepared fresh. Some leaders, sensing our distrust in big church and a desire for intimacy, have called for doing away with a collective Sunday experience altogether and returning to a house-church model. A potluck experience in which we all contribute. And other churches, it seems, are working overtime to build brand loyalty with digital natives through an aggressive social media presence, polished graphics, and tweetable sermons. "Hello Fresh" church comes right to your door with the ingredients already cut and measured, no work required. During the Covid-19 pandemic, all churches have had to learn a virtual language. I wonder what will become of our mother tongue.

Can the underlying Sunday-service values that my mom instilled in me—authenticity, excellence, liveness, creativity, and intentionality—still guide us, even if the aesthetic shifts? What if beauty was never the problem? Could it actually *help* to welcome those brave young souls who would dare set foot inside a place they fear is unsafe? How might beauty build trust? And, for the cynics with good reason to retreat, what might we discover through our presence?

Because I still long to be invited to a feast. What meal can compare to the banquet of a great host, who has thought through the seating, the courses, and toasts at a table open to all?

Taking on a Christmas project here or there led to further creative partnerships with churches across the country. What began for me as an accidental and sort of nostalgic side hustle grew into a great passion of mine—creating artistic content for churches. And regardless of the size of the audience, the sanctuary, or the denomination, there are certain core principles I am learning to rely on.

The element of surprise. "I have come to greatly appreciate the importance of the element of surprise in cracking through people's barriers," writes Michelle Hensley in *All the Lights On*. Michelle is an innovative theater artist who is bringing the form to audiences that traditional theaters exclude. When she brings plays to prisons, rural towns, housing projects, and chemical-dependency treatment centers, her audiences often have a well-founded suspicion that theater is not for them, and these learned attitudes must be attended to in the first moments of the show.

My mom and I had the privilege of traveling to Australia and New Zealand for a series of conferences about men and women working well together. It was an uncomfortable topic in an uncomfortable setting since many of those in the room would represent churches with different viewpoints on gender roles. It was also coming on the heels of the #ChurchToo movement that had revealed terrible stories of abuse within ministry settings, including a high-profile story involving my mom. Yikes!

How could we begin such a gathering? What would be the right tone to set? How could we gently encourage people to let their guards down?

I was surprised when Mom called me one day, as we were preparing, to say she thought we should start with something humorous. "There will be so much tension in the room before we begin," she said. "What if we just let people laugh?" I followed her logic, but I was also nervous. At the core this wasn't a funny subject at all. There would be women in the room with trauma suffered from sexism and abuse in ministry. If we wanted them to laugh, we needed to be sure they were laughing about the right thing.

We decided to have fun with the absurdity of the rules that churches were putting into place where men and women are working together. At the very start of the session I came out wearing a red blow-up suit that made me look five times my size. Pretending to be a conference attendee, I revealed that my fictional church was requiring all the women to wear these so that no one would be tempted to sin. The piece named some other heightened, ridiculous rules we dreamed up, which got people laughing, and eventually it landed in a tender place where the character reaffirms that she is still there—despite how hard her church has made it for her—she still feels called to ministry. Then my mom walked into the tension of that moment and began to share her wisdom on how we can navigate this together constructively.

Even after the first few times we did it, it felt like a risk every single time I turned on my little whirring fan inside my red blow-up suit and walked in to start the conference in a new city. Maybe we have to get more accustomed to this scary feeling. It *is* risky to deviate from expectations, and we will certainly fail sometimes. But when an artistic risk pays off, it stays with us long after the experience. In this instance it wasn't any of the words I spoke but the blow-up suit that people remember. "That's exactly how it feels," one woman said. "That's how we're supposed to approach ministry as women: disembodied." We had found a singular image that revealed a deep truth.

The language of metaphor. As far as I can see, metaphor is the boat that has carried the Christian tradition forward. It's what holds up across centuries, bridging languages, people, and places. It's the container that helps us understand and express our identity in Christ and our purpose in the world. The image of a lost sheep unlocks something universal and true. God as Father gives us some sure footing inside of that which we cannot comprehend: his presence available to us as bread and wine, the Spirit as fluid as wind, the bride of Christ, the waters of baptism. These ancient symbols link us to deep truth: longing and mystery far better than wordy, technical explanations.

Sometimes, the right image can unlock something in us that we could never reach on a road built of words.

When I was a teenager I attended a church service about forgiveness. After the message the music team played a thematically connected song. A few lines into the song a man walked onstage carrying a heavy suitcase. He paused, set it down, and walked off.

Soon a woman came forward, dragging her own piece of luggage. She too abandoned it and walked off. More and more people came forward until there was a pile of suitcases onstage. It was a stunning visual reminder of how holding on to a grudge becomes a burden to us. They found the perfect, evocative image. When I think of resentment, I still think of a suitcase.

No spectacle without substance. The equal and opposite danger of completely ignoring the power of imagery is putting all resources into a flash of visual intensity without fleshing out the meaning or the connective tissue that prepares us for such a sensory overload. In other words, I have yet to be moved by an aerialist in a Christmas service. And I have seen a lot of aerialists in Christmas services.

I always appreciate the effort to incorporate creative elements. But we harness the power of art when we marry form and function, connecting spectacular moments into the deeper meaning or question of the service. No matter how talented they are, the drumline, the aerialist, and the dance team will feel random and, worst of all, *thin* if they are disconnected from the other elements and no one builds on or unpacks the imagery. My playwriting professor, Laura, used to talk about palette. Everything you put into your story—or, I would argue, a service—becomes a part of the palette. If you introduce too many colors or textures or themes or metaphors, it gets muddy.

The steady accumulation of suitcases was a spectacle moment—visually arresting and awe-inspiring because it built so naturally on all that had come before it, but the moment took us somewhere we couldn't have seen coming. It was not seductive, glamorous, sexy, or expensive. It was *resonant*.

Staying in the storm. Perhaps, above all else, art can help build trust by meeting us in our mess. In *And Then You Act: Making Art in an Unpredictable World*, renowned theater director

Anne Bogart says, "The artist's job is to stay alive and awake in the space between convictions and certainties." It is this space of mystery, doubt, and tension that I wish more Sundays would take me to or meet me in. Because this is the space where life actually happens, where faith is truly born. Though preachers do their best to honor and name the trials we face, because we see them as *teacher* we know there is a lesson coming on the other side of the relatable story or the provocative questions. Artists bear no such burden. They can stand squarely in the middle of the muck and in doing so, honor our rage, our suspicion, our longings, our missteps, our fears, and our fancies. If an audience feels that these parts of them are safe, perhaps they will listen to what happens next.

In his book *Telling the Truth*, Frederick Buechner writes,

> There would be a strong argument for saying that much of the most powerful preaching of our time is the preaching of the poets, playwrights, novelists because it is often they better than the rest of us who speak with awful honesty about the absence of God in the world and about the storm of his absence, both without and within, which, because it is unendurable, unlivable, drives us to look to the eye of the storm.

One Christmas I crafted a story in three parts. A sister betrays her siblings in part 2 and the siblings forgive her in part 3, which the audience is invited to imagine takes place many years later. Something about how it all stacked together never felt quite right to me, even after hours of rehearsal and editing. It wasn't until a friend came to the service that she gently helped me see what I had missed. "I couldn't help but wonder what took place in between the last two parts," she said. In jumping ahead to tie up the story with a big Christmas bow, I had missed an opportunity to show the characters wrestling with their resentment and doing the hard work that leads to forgiveness. We skipped the better, harder story in part 2.5.

The reverence of approach. The service designed by the team is like the birthday kid's house decked out in balloons, appetizers, and donkeys hung up without tails. It's not a party without the people and their participation. It is we—the ones who might have slept in, the ones who fought during the whole car ride, the ones who haven't had a moment all week to see deeper than the problems and tasks right in front of our faces—who complete the experience. It is the collision of our presence and the Spirit that builds the blueprint the team has thoughtfully prepared.

Brené Brown writes about the importance of collective assembly in her book *Braving the Wilderness*:

> Collective assembly has long been a part of the human experience. . . . Collective assembly is more than just people coming together to distract themselves from life by watching a game, concert, or play—instead it is an opportunity to feel connected to something bigger than oneself; it is an opportunity to feel joy, social connection, meaning, and peace.

There is something that happens when we emerge from the particulars of our individual and collective suffering to remember the cycle of death and redemption together. And I believe the embodied act of that emergence holds great power. In his book *On Beauty*, writer John O'Donohue calls this "the reverence of approach" and reflects on how this has collapsed in the age of digital distraction when we jump from one experience, image, or idea to the next, fast as we can click:

> What you encounter, recognize or discover depends to a large degree on the quality of your approach. Because we have lost reverence of approach, we should not be too

surprised at the lack of quality and beauty in our experience. . . . A gracious approach is the key that unlocks the treasure of encounter. . . . A reverence of approach awakens depth and enables us to be truly present where we are. The rushed heart and the arrogant mind lack the gentleness and pa-tience to enter that embrace.

I don't think this means you can't fight the whole car ride to church and still experience depth. But I do wonder if the car ride itself matters. The reverence lies not in our attempts to construct some holy state of mind but in the embodied journey and partici-pation in the sacraments in the context of community. When we attend a wedding, we are preparing ourselves to be moved by the ceremony in all the acts leading up to it: when we purchase the present, board the plane, get dressed up, and do all the work of bringing our bodies to the moment. I'm in that season of life when all of my friends decided to get married at once, and every time an invitation arrives my husband and I worry whether we can afford it and if it's worth the effort. And every single time we witness two people declaring their love for one another in front of their village, every time we cry and toast and laugh and dance and remember our commitment to each other, we come home and say to each other, "I'm so glad we went." We extended our-selves deeply and we experienced something deeply in return.

I hope that those who wonder if church has anything left to offer them offer enough of themselves to truly see. And I hope churches will resist the temptation to move away from moments that require the community's presence and participation. The sermon podcast may be a great starting place, but it is only a sliver of the expression. We cannot think our way into an em-bodied expression of love.

And if we do give the gift of our attention and our tired bodies, if we put on pants with a zipper and fight off the shiny screens that promise infinitely easier invitations, will it matter that we did? If we choose not to numb, what will we feel? If we choose to *go*, welcome us, grip us, delight us, soothe us, see us, inspire us, touch us—just don't leave us the same.

———

In her book *The Art of Gathering*, Priya Parker reflects not just on our approach to an event but also on our journey back into the world. These "threshold moments," she argues, are as important as what transpires in between them.

When I left big, nondenominational churches for a Methodist church in Austin, I honestly wondered if art had any role to play in this more traditional, small-church context. We meet in an old building with stained-glass windows and the teaching follows the lectionary. There are liturgical prayers and Communion every week. But the creative way in which they send people back across the threshold into our private lives demonstrates how art can still function powerfully when adapted to fit the aesthetic of the place.

The pastor, Jason, had a desire to incorporate more creative elements into their services, not just for the sake of doing so but to invite his congregation to imaginative places that teaching alone could not take them. Jason looked around at who he already had in his small congregation. Mark had served in many ways throughout the church, but never out of his primary gifting and passion—poetry. They decided to experiment with Mark writing custom benedictions each weekend that were in conversation with the sermon, the music, and the themes of that service. These short poems became the bridge, as any good benediction is, between the time we spend together in worship and the world we enter back into. After each service the church posted the benedictions online, a reminder of what we had experienced together and how we might carry it forward.

Three years later the benedictions are a treasured part of the Sunday service. A whole team of poets has come out of the woodwork, and now, under Mark's leadership, each writer contributes their gift. If ever they are late in posting the poem, people ask for it, longing to once again engage with this piece of art they have learned to treasure.

Barbara Brown Taylor goes so far as to suggest that "the church's central task is an imaginative one." In her book *The Preaching Life*, she writes,

> In the imaginative act, we are grasped whole. Revelation is not a matter of thinking or feeling, intuiting or sensing, working from the left side of the brain or the right. It is a shocking gift of new sight that obliterates such distinctions, grabbing us by our lapels and turning us around, so that when we are set back down again we see everything from a new angle. We reason differently, feel differently, act differently. Imagination does more than affect us; it effects change in our lives.

When a church deploys its artists to do what they do best, Sundays can be not just a thing of beauty but an invitation to a new world.

A year and a half of Covid-19 has given us all the gift of new sight. It has demanded that we all answer a new question on Sundays: Well, what if you *can't* be there? Then what?

This has collapsed some of the categories we clung to, expanding our definition of church and the Sunday gathering in particular, out and beyond our physical buildings and the experiences that happen there. Through new remote church members I am beginning to see that the local church has always been a micro-expression of universal truths. Taking Communion on my couch has reminded me that everything is sacred, and there was nothing magic in the cups underneath the stained glass.

My friend César planted a church during the pandemic. His dream to create an inclusive Latino faith community in Austin transformed into something he could not have imagined: an inclusive Latino faith community spanning most of the Spanish-speaking world. This particular expression is becoming known for its wide-open table, the courage to ask hard questions, and a liberating spirit that gathers around the gospel that sets people free. Unable to find a Spanish-speaking community quite like this in their context, people from all over Latin America, Europe, and the United States call Amor Original—a community without a physical building or gathering—their church. Many members communicate daily on a WhatsApp group, encouraging and supporting one another from miles away.

César says, "We've had to really define what being together is. Jesus tells us that where two or three gathered in my name, there I am with them. So, where is the Holy Spirit when you gather online? In the cords, in the screens, the Wi-Fi waves traveling between us? I don't know, but we are promised of his presence."

Honestly, watching Amor Original flourish has challenged my most treasured ideas about Sundays. As a theater-maker and even as a recovering daughter of the megachurch movement, I have an enormous bias toward the three-dimensional gathering. Perhaps this makes me an unreliable narrator, but I will always believe in what happens when we sit, stand, and sing side by side. And I think churches have overestimated the extent to which my generation would prefer to engage online, creating snack-sized content and a social media presence that feels more sales-y than soul-sized.

But if we come together on Sundays to glimpse the heaven on earth that we're building together, maybe there are far more possibilities than I once thought as to how the Holy Spirit can move us to a new vision. Yes, maybe the Spirit shows up in creative expressions that surprise, grip, and enchant us. Maybe the Spirit shows up in our strange and timeworn sacraments, communal embodiments that tomorrow's church need not outrun in favor of slick screens and tweetable truths. And maybe also, at the same time, the Spirit is moving across oceans, through cable lines and networks, whispering of a future in which we see we were never as alone as we feared.

5

When Harry Works with Sally

Men and Women Leading Well Together

NANCY

Once upon a time, long before cell phones, automobiles, Twitter, or fast food, a leader assigned to someone a vitally important job. The mission required traveling a long distance to deliver one of the most significant letters ever written. The person with the letter would be expected to do far more than simply drop off the document and dash. The carrier of the letter had to be fully prepared and equipped to offer explanations and perspectives on the challenging content found there. The leader wrote a preface to the future hearers, commending the messenger as someone who should be listened to and respected. This mission was a big deal.

The leader who made the pivotal assignment was the apostle Paul. And the person he chose to carry the weight of this massive responsibility—to deliver and defend arguably the most theologically rich of all of Paul's letters—was a woman named Phoebe. Reading the final chapter of the letter to the Romans, what stands out vividly is that Paul worked with an outstanding team of men and women. He called them out by name, and in many cases affirmed them for specific contributions to the ministry. The first two verses offer us the only mention of Phoebe in the Bible. Yet in just about fifty words Paul revealed vital information about this remarkable leader, writing,

> I commend you to our sister Phoebe, a deacon of the church in Cenchreae. I ask you to receive her in the Lord in a way worthy of his people and to give her any help she may need from you, for she has been the benefactor of many people, including me. (Romans 16:1-2)

First, a little background. Paul is sending a letter to the Romans from Corinth, a center of business in Greece. Corinth was a thriving city full of traders, travelers, and sailors at the crossroads between Asia and Europe. Phoebe was a part of a lively Christian congregation in Cenchreae, a port city about six or eight miles outside of Corinth. What exactly did Phoebe do in that church? In the original Greek language Paul chose the word *diakonos*, from which we get our word *deacon*. It is very telling that when it comes to translating *diakonos* to describe male leaders, it is almost always translated as "minister" or "deacon." But to describe Phoebe, the English word chosen by some English translations (e.g., ESV, NASB, NKJV, KJV) is "servant." Nothing wrong, of course, with being a servant. But scholars generally agree that Phoebe had a recognized ministry and responsibility in her local church. She was a leader. Phoebe also served as a benefactor of the church, which tells us she was a woman of means, possibly an astute businesswoman who allowed the church to meet in her home.

Paul chose to send Phoebe on an eight hundred-mile journey to Rome. There she would deliver his letter, likely reading it aloud to the believers and then fielding questions about the content. Paul tells the Romans that he "commends" Phoebe to them, giving her a vote of confidence and his enthusiastic endorsement.

But another word jumps out to me. Notice that Paul calls Phoebe his "sister." Using this word to describe a spiritual relationship, Paul also calls some of his male coworkers his "brothers." In their book, *A Church Called Tov*, Scot McKnight and Laura Barringer tell us that the most common word in the New Testament for Christian believers—by far—is not *church*. It is *siblings* or *brothers and sisters*.

Paul's vision was remarkably progressive for his day: Within the body of Christ, he says, we are to consider one another no longer according to social status, ethnic status, or gendered status. "There is no longer Jew or Gentile, slave or free, male and female. For you are all one in Christ Jesus." That is, we are all siblings.

Paul knew from experience the richness of sharing leadership with both men and women. He was honoring all his ministry partners, regardless of gender. And we see in the early church a beautiful picture of how God intended for us to serve him together in the context of rich community as brothers and sisters in his forever family.

Sounds great. But sadly, this vision of goodness, of seeing one another as brothers and sisters, has been broken in far too many of our churches. The wonder of partnership, as I believe God intended for it to be lived out among us, is not the experience of many. In his book *Healing America's Wounds*, John Dawson writes, "The wounds inflicted by men and women on each other constitute the fundamental fault line running beneath all other human conflict. . . . It is the biggest reconciliation issue of all outside of our need to be reconciled to God."

I believe that every human has a God-given deep desire for healthy brother and sister relationships where we feel known, supported, understood, and challenged by friendships with both genders. Where does this all go terribly wrong?

———

March 23, 2018. My birthday. In sunny Florida with my husband on a long-planned vacation. I awoke to the online version of the *Chicago Tribune*, reading an article I already knew was coming, seeing my name in print as one of several women reporting a wide range of inappropriate behavior by our senior pastor. Going back to 2014, I heard from a reliable source that a woman I knew from Willow had reported specific allegations of a fourteen-year affair with Bill Hybels. Many months later she stated that her story was made up and refused to talk about it any further. But her initial confession brought to light reports of other experiences of harassment or abuse of power, eventually including ten women.

When I first heard the reports, like most people who have been greatly influenced by Bill, I did not want to believe it. After all, this was the pastor who had opened up doors of opportunity for me and other women to fully express our gifts in the church. He was a fierce advocate for women leaders, inviting us to be included in every circle in the church. I am fully aware that Bill invested in my leadership development and launched me into significant roles, including being the first female teaching pastor of the church. With a front-row seat to Bill's phenomenal influence on both Willow and countless other churches around the world, I did not want to believe there was a dark side, though I had hints along the way (In chapter seven I will explore some reflections on how it can be possible for leaders—really, for any of us—to walk closely with God, bear much fruit, and then make terrible choices of sin that harm so many.)

As more reports from women came to light, I looked back and could see moments in Bill's behavior, including with me, that had crossed the line of what one expects from her pastor. When some other brave women came forward who had more significant tales to tell, I recognized that my own story had been part of a pattern over time, a pattern that spanned almost three decades—Bill flirting with or grooming women, most of us on staff or leaders he met through the church.

I joined a small group of advocates, all six of us former key leaders from the church, who began a process trying to bring information to the elders so they could further investigate. We also sought for over a year to meet with Bill, but he refused. In 2016 we met with five of the elders. By that time they believed they had done enough investigation and had cleared Bill's name. We implored them to dig deeper and to hire a truly independent investigative team.

The story from there is a long and complex one. Of course, I am writing my version, stemming from my limited perspective. It's easy to think there were obvious right answers or for me to label myself and others as heroes, victims, or villains. I suspect most everyone involved would love a do-over on the entire process. But the advocates came to a choice: we could let this go and allow Bill to retire as planned (which was not full retirement, as he intended to continue teaching through the Willow Creek Association), or we could go to the press. I seriously wondered if we should let it go because I truly did not want to severely damage the ministry of the church worldwide. But then I heard about another, more recent, story of Bill's inappropriate behavior with a young woman on staff. This pattern of sin had to be stopped. And the church had to be known as a place where abuse of women and abuse of power would not be tolerated. So I joined in a decision to go to the press because we did not see any other option to bring the truth to light. My intent with the *Tribune* reporters all along was to be "off the record." I did not want my name in print. But as publication of the article was looming, the two reporters came to our home, showed us what they hoped to write, and asked me one more time if I would allow them to use my name. I looked at my husband and then simply said we would think it over and pray about it. A few days later Warren said to me, "Honey, this is totally your decision. But for whatever it's worth, I think it might be important for you to let them give your name." And while I had some sense of the storm this would stir up, I chose to offer my name in support of the other women.

Back in Florida, on March 23, I walked the beach with a heavy heart, toes digging into the hot sand, leaving my phone for a few hours to ignore the multitude of messages. The rest of this story is so very sad. After two "family meetings" conducted at the church to essentially defend Bill and call all of us "colluders" and "liars," Bill eventually resigned, admitting very little. A few months later, after a major article in the *New York Times* described another tragic tale of a woman who came forward, all of the elders and the new lead pastor also resigned.

On the morning after those resignations, I walked down my driveway to pick up our daily *Tribune* and saw another front-page story about Willow. My heart was breaking. How did it come to this? What would happen to the church I loved? How would any of the broken relationships ever be repaired? How would the women who were victims be healed? And what would happen to the future partnerships of women and men in local churches around the world? This was not how any of us who helped to build Willow Creek would have ever wanted the story to go. I just wanted to weep.

The tragedy of my former church took place in the context of a dramatic moment in our culture that has brought to light accusations of the abuse of power and sexual misconduct of leaders in entertainment, academia, sports, business, and, yes, also the church. So many stories connected to the Me Too/Church Too movement compel many of us to wonder if it is possible for men and women to serve, lead, and work together with love and respect—without it eventually leading to moral failures. I read a *Wall Street Journal* headline from December 3, 2018, that advised men to "Simply Avoid Women at All Costs!" I find myself carrying a heavy weight of concern that all the examples of sin will lead to an overreaction where men and women feel so afraid and awkward that we run to our separate corners. The church worldwide often responds with a sort of Puritan approach, erecting a huge barricade between men and women, setting up twenty new rules about how we can never be alone together with someone from the opposite sex in an elevator, a car, an office, or a restaurant. These rules make it even more difficult for women to lead, to do our job.

In a *Christianity Today* article titled "When Moral Boundaries Become Incubators for Sin," Amy Simpson says that too often rigid systems don't work and boundaries can serve as medication, making us think we are safe. Healthy boundaries, she says, "produce lasting change only in partnership with God's protection and the kind of work that causes inner transformation and growth." Is there another path forward? To that question, I proclaim a resounding *yes!* Our God has designed a far better way for men and women to flourish together in work and ministry, to experience the brotherhood and sisterhood modeled in the early church and taught by Paul and Peter. How can each of us, male and female, do our part to create God-honoring partnerships?

I believe we begin by *knowing the story we bring* to this moment. Every individual ushers in our own background to issues of gender. We have a lens or a perspective that was forged first in the home where we grew up, then in our school experience, our earliest jobs, and our key relationships.

Here's a brief window into some of my story. I grew up as a baby boomer in a family in which my mom did not work outside the home. She also did not volunteer anywhere or have a car at her disposal. She was always home. Growing up, my bright and intelligent mom had no opportunity to go to college or pursue a career. This was the picture I saw day after day as a young girl.

The wonderful church we attended was led almost entirely by men. Up front on Sunday morning, men preached and led worship and made announcements. The top leaders sat in chairs that looked like ivory thrones lined up in front of the choir loft. Men at that church could become *deacons*. My dad was a deacon.

Women were *deaconesses*, and their role was to provide mercy and hospitality, especially to the grieving. Women did not serve on the boards that made any of the strategic decisions in the church. I did see women lead in the children's ministry and knew that they could lead Bible studies for other women. But women did not lead grown men unless they were missionaries overseas.

I began to wonder if something was wrong with me, if a mistake had been made when I was assigned my gifts. At school I expressed leadership gifts. I was voted president of the student council, competed on speech teams, and led in the theater department. But I wondered if I could ever lead in a church setting, if I could ever use the gifts God gave me to make a difference there and to influence the lives of both men and women. In high school and college I assumed I would leverage my influence somewhere in the secular world, likely in the media business.

What is your story when it comes to gender? What did you see in your home? If you had two parents in the home, were your parents coequal partners, or was your experience more traditional? If you grew up going to church, what did you see there? In your work experience have you ever reported to a female boss? All of this matters more than we know because it's part of our story and what we grow to be comfortable with, what we think of as normal.

The formation of our perspective on gender includes, of course, our theological view, what we have been taught about Scripture, and the position we have adopted or chosen spanning from an egalitarian position (seeing each role in the church as open to both men and women) to a complementarian view, which limits the roles women can play, often drawing the line at elders or teaching pastors. But I also see that our theology is only one part of our story—our comfort level or past experiences influence us as well. A friend of mine served in the young-adults ministry of a large church. She had the privilege of helping to lead a young woman to Christ. When it came time for baptism, that new believer asked if my friend could baptize her. Up until that time only men had done baptisms in their church. My friend met with the senior pastor with the request. He carefully thought about it and admitted to her that he had no theological reason why a woman couldn't baptize. He said it was just outside his comfort zone because he'd never really seen it before. His hesitation was not about theology but was based on his past story. He nonetheless decided to allow my friend to perform the baptism.

I urge you to reflect for a moment on your own story and to explore and dig for any unconscious bias you may carry toward the other sex. We also need to acknowledge that when we look at our past, for some there are deep wounds. Maybe, whether you are male or female, you have been hurt by the abusive power of another leader. Experts also tell us that our congregations and workplaces are filled with survivors of sexual abuse, that more than half of all women have experienced unwanted and inappropriate sexual advances, and that one in four girls and one in six boys will be sexually abused before they turn eighteen. To move forward, these sisters and brothers need to find opportunities to lament, grieve, and heal over time, seeking truth and grace. And hopefully, victims will find the church to be a safe place to process their wounds, to be believed and supported.

———

Once we know the story we bring and do our own inner work, I believe the better way calls us to three major commitments.

The commitment to soul care. To avoid the dangers of moral failure or the abuse of power requires us to pay far more attention to the state of our souls—cooperating with the work of God to transform us and lead us away from our shadow sides. With the rapid pace of life, too many of us focus on what we are *doing* for God rather than on who we are *becoming*. Yes, I'm talking about the work of spiritual formation, preferably in the context of a loving and truthful community. We talk a lot about accountability, but the truth is that accountability only works when we choose to be honest. And most of us are good at hiding. I began a journey about ten years ago of understanding and admitting my capacity for hiding and pretending, for crafting an image that I am more together, more spiritual, than I truly am. As each of us pays attention to the state of our soul, we will be able to move past our fear and engage in healthy relationships with brothers and sisters. Ruth Haley Barton describes this kind of community in her book *Equal to the Task*:

> Imagine a setting where respect for fellow human beings is so vibrant and so real that it feeds people's souls. . . . What kind of person would you be if you were to treat others as though they were sacred and precious? What difference would it make if women and men were to approach each other with this kind of wonder and care? Though it may sound simplistic, there is a real possibility that if women and men learned to respect each other deeply—to see each other as the ones through whom God is made present among us—little else would be needed.

As we invite Christ to make his home in us, it becomes unthinkable to treat any person as a sexual object. We become so surrendered to Jesus that we treasure the opportunity to truly love one another as brothers and sisters, and to labor together for the cause of our faith.

We must also ground our relationships with faithfulness to the Scriptures that teach us to be kind, forgiving, truthful, and honoring to one another. I am always inspired by reflecting on how countercultural Jesus was in his behavior toward women. He valued them, spoke to them with respect, and even trusted the miraculous moment of his resurrection to the witness—primarily first—of women.

The commitment to honest conversations. Cathy, a woman who plays a senior leadership role in a thriving Midwestern church, joined one of my coaching circles several years ago. At one point when our group was exploring what it means to find our voice in ministry, Cathy shared that she knew God was prompting her to initiate a difficult conversation with her executive pastor. As in many churches, all the salary information for their staff was secret and highly confidential. Cathy carried a hunch that the women on their staff who had similar roles to some of the men were possibly underpaid. Once Cathy was promoted to a new role as overall family minister, she was invited to see the salary information for the departments that now reported to her. Cathy discovered that the situation was even worse than she feared—a far-too-large salary gap that was related to gender. Our circle supported and prayed for Cathy as she scheduled the candid conversation she knew was necessary with her executive pastor. To his credit he listened well, agreed with her assessment, and launched a rigorous overview of their salary structure, leading to major adjustments and equity over time.

Candid conversations are essential if we are ever going to see the gender divide made healthy and whole. This begins with an honest assessment of the current reality—what are men and women experiencing in your church culture as they seek to partner with one another? On a scale of one to ten, how healthy do you think your culture is for men and women working together? Is it possible you have a lack of knowledge as to what others are experiencing?

If you are a male leader, I encourage you to invite a few women with leadership gifts to meet with you and ask them some key questions about their experience on your team. Essentially, you want to know what it's like for them in your environment, to help you understand. If you have the maturity and courage to ask the questions, your job is then to be quiet and not get defensive. Listen well. I guarantee if you initiate this dialogue, your sense of urgency about the issue of men and women working well together will increase. We cannot address what we do not know about.

The commitment to intentionally develop women leaders. At what age, in the course of her entire life, do you think a woman peaks in terms of her confidence? Twenty-five? Forty-seven? Sixty-three? All those answers are *wrong*. The right answer is nine! A young girl is hopeful and confident that what she thinks and does matters, that she can truly make a difference. I know I felt that kind of bold energy at age nine. Canadian researcher and writer Ellen Duffield has explored this question in-depth and believes that after nine, most women drift toward insecurity.

I learned about Ellen and her work from Pastor Jeff Lockyer, who I referenced in chapter three. According to their theology, Southridge Church is egalitarian. But about six years ago Jeff says he and other senior leaders realized that despite their biblical position, there were no women on their senior leadership team or communicating regularly on Sunday mornings. So they began to do a lot of listening and chose to become highly intentional. They decided to make a *disproportionate investment into female leadership*. This includes training and skills development for adult women but also a fantastic program for middle school girls called BRAVE, involving three years of building into girls' lives, seeing their gifts and potential, and training them for leadership.

Second, they decided to make a *disproportionate invitation for female leadership*. Their goal is to see women in at least 30 percent of the key leadership levels. Currently, Southridge has female elders, and their board chair is female along with 50 percent of their staff. They are also gaining ground with up-front female communicators and teachers. None of this would happen without intentionality.

Did you know that it's extremely difficult for a young girl to become what she cannot see? One of my prized memories from my years as a teaching pastor at Willow was a moment after I had taught on a Sunday morning. A mom and her young daughter, a girl around age seven, stood in line to talk to me after the service. The mom explained that the girl sometimes liked to draw or doodle during church—I certainly remember doing the same growing up. Then the daughter, with a shy smile, gave me the picture she drew on a piece of red paper. The drawing featured a podium with a stick figure, clearly a woman, standing behind it, holding up her arms. The woman sported a bob hairstyle like mine. I kept the picture to remind myself that young eyes—both girls and boys—are watching. I could never have drawn that kind of picture as a child. But I'm thrilled to see a shift emerging, slowly in some cases, in many churches where women are intentionally developed and seen and invited to the table of leadership and the podium of preaching.

———

I have one biological brother. His name is Chip, and we have always been advocates for each other. But I have several other brothers in Christ who I am deeply grateful for. They include Steve, Rory, Greg, John, Jimmy, Doug, Fred, Joe, Dan, and another guy named Chip. Without these brothers I would be less of the person God called me to be. I know these guys would all join me in announcing that a great cloud of witnesses down through history shout out to us today, "You can do this!" All the way back to Adam and Eve, Miriam and Moses, Deborah and Barak, Esther and Mordecai, Priscilla and Aquila, Paul and Phoebe. Let's not allow our fear to prevent us from the vision God designed for us to serve side by side, sisters and brothers who respectfully and lovingly build the kingdom on earth together.

SAMANTHA

"The *Quiet and Gentle Spirit* award goes to Samantha Beach!" My heart sank. I would have rather not gotten a medal at all. Quiet and gentle in Spirit! I had poured my heart into camp that summer: every morning I left it all on the floor in my basketball specialty, dripping from running sprints in the Southern 100-degree heat. I was the clown of my cabin, and I lived for rainy days when classes were canceled and I could lead our group in making up skits and songs. I was a determined learner and always got the day's memory verse down by lunchtime. I felt wild, strong, focused, funny, and free. But Christian camp told me I was quiet and gentle.

Then it came time for them to announce the award for the boys' side of camp. Some floppy-haired Payton or Taylor or Walker came up to receive it, the highest honor boys could receive, the male equivalent—or complement—to a quiet and gentle spirit: the Lion Heart award.

———

I remember hearing Mom practice her messages behind the door of her office, down the hall from my room. I would linger quietly near her door, craning my head to hear more. She would use a different part of her voice: deeper, authoritative, but still tender. It was not the same voice that called me to breakfast or cheered for me to score a lay-up. Neither was it performative or inauthentic. It was just . . . pastoral. To catch her practicing at home was kind of like seeing a teacher at the grocery store. Jarring, awkward, and yet entrancing. Who are you when you're not the you that you are to me?

Later she would ask my dad for jokes. He could always be counted on to come up with a quip about the snow or the Bears losing (in TV, they call it giving the script a punch-up). Mom would walk downstairs and Dad would give her sermon a one-man punch-up.

My sister and I had two jobs, and we took these roles very seriously: first, to grant permission for our names and stories to be used in a sermon illustration (to maintain my power, I always pretended to think it over, but I can't ever remember saying no to secondhand spotlight); and second, outfit and jewelry selection. Mom would present a few clothing options, and we always had to consider the pattern (Too busy on screen?), the cut (Was this tank top worth the emails of wives worried about their distracted husbands?), the shoes (Would heels be tricky climbing the steps? But were these pants made to go with flats?), and the dangly factor of the earrings (Would they interfere with the mic?). I took my jobs very seriously. I sensed that male pastors had less to worry about.

I can hardly remember a message my mom taught without getting emotional. Sometimes it was just a glimmer of a tear, but it always came. It was just a matter of when. Dad would whisper, lovingly, "Here she goes!" As if every sermon she lowered a basket of words deeper and deeper down a well until finally she broke the surface, cleansing us in connection and resonance. Her tears made me uncomfortable. No one likes to see their mom cry. But they were always genuine. Her way of saying "this matters" or "can you believe it?" And the people were eager to listen.

Anyone who's regularly in front of a congregation of twenty thousand is something of a celebrity in a sleepy suburb. We would get stopped at restaurants and in the parking lot by women *and* men thanking her for her words. And often specifically for her vulnerability. Her messages were full of wisdom and intellectual depth, but there was something unique that she brought to this cerebral craft. You cannot escape her teaching with your heart intact.

I grew up seeing women onstage pretty regularly, and, as with the arts in church, I didn't realize this was an anomaly until adulthood. Nancy O. had a rhythm that soothed until it stirred, and I loved how she used her hands to communicate like she was conducting an orchestra of ideas. Jeanne's ferocity radiates out of her until it awakens something wild in you. Today, I get to hear regularly from women in my church. Jen makes us laugh until the whole room feels like family. Esha's legal mind could persuade me to jump out of a plane, but fortunately she employs her rhetorical skills to inspire greater generosity and social activism. And no one can nurture nuance like Jessica, while boldly inviting me deeper into the vast mystery of God. When I've been part of churches where the teaching is mostly handled by That Guy, and sometimes That Other Guy, I am saddened by the implicit agreement made by all who gather there: that the image of God made manifest in women has less to teach us. We would content ourselves with an obstructed view of the divine.

One year the Promiseland drama team brought the Christmas story to life in a twenty-five-minute interactive, dramatic retelling for the kids' ministries. I was cast as Mary opposite a Joseph I had worked with a lot. He and I were cast together often—we had played siblings, talk-show hosts, rappers, best friends, and superheroes. He was my pal and could always be counted on to make me laugh, gross me out, or find a great new hiding spot when we played Sardines in the food court.

But that weekend everything changed. The camera in the freight elevator caught my Joseph making out with the angel between services. The other kids came rushing into the green room saying, "Did you hear? Is there any place in this building that *doesn't* have a camera? What do you think the director will say?" I tried not to be offended that my Joseph had strayed. The angel costume of the kissed girl was very pretty compared to my homely Mary look. Like any good actor, I used my pain to inform my work. The Saturday 7:00 p.m. service Mary knew betrayal in a way that the 5:00 p.m. Mary simply did not.

I remember sensing that something had shifted after the great elevator incident of 2003. We were teenagers now. And serving together, boys and girls becoming men and women, wouldn't be quite so simple anymore.

But we weren't sent to separate corners. We got to collaborate again and again. We played friends asking hard questions, we learned dances when our changing bodies would rather melt into the wall, and one time my friend Trent and I taught onstage together as high schoolers about love, lust, and body image (being experts, of course, on all of these things). I will always be grateful for the adult leaders who empowered these formative collaborations, modeled leaning into the stickiness, and taught me that we were most creative, most dynamic, and most effective as a team when we partnered together as brothers and sisters.

I saw these partnerships at the highest level in our church. So, it was shocking, years later, to learn what I hadn't seen.

———

The stories of sexual misconduct and abuse of power that my mom and other women shared created a logic puzzle I could not crack. How much did I have to release to make room for this revelation? Does the exposure of a leader render their followers to be fools? Was the teaching less true? Was the impact of Willow meaningless? How could a leader live a lie and the Jesus he spoke of be true and transformative? There were no answers, only more questions. Each question is a door to a hallway full of doors. Where would this end? Could I ever find my way back?

At once, I wanted to return everything Willow had given me. And, with equal desire and desperation, I wanted to cling to that which was good. I wanted it still to be good.

The members of the congregation wrestled with these same questions. It is a near-impossible thing to accept that a spiritual leader who has facilitated your flourishing has caused irreparable harm to others. And many simply did not accept it.

After the story broke in the *Chicago Tribune*, I graduated from head necklace picker-outer to managing my mom's social media account. I didn't ever speak for her (though she does need some handholding when posting, especially if she has to do something high-tech, like tag someone), but I had first eyes on her inbox. I was the bouncer, and I threw out those who came only to wound before she would ever have to see them. I saw them though.

I had always imagined that the hateful, judgmental Christians were "out there." I'd see them on the news or online and think, *How embarrassing. They don't know the real Jesus at all.* I gathered "cool Christians" around me like a protective blanket, lulling me into believing our brand of faith was soft and not sharp; warm, not piercing; safe, never savage. But when I saw my people, our people, spew such vitriol, when I saw the church my mom helped build disbelieve, discredit, and dismiss her story—all while I reckoned with my own binary thinking—it became clear that the sickness of certainty had spread close to home.

How could we imagine that *every other industry* in our world was reckoning with the legacy of abuse and power that has run unchecked but *the church would be somehow exempt*? Oh, we wish it were so, but we know our transformation isn't complete. That's why we show up every Sunday! And the church has been wedded to patriarchy as intimately as any other institution in America. Where other fields have made great strides toward the inclusion of women leaders, Barna Research found that in 2017 women hold a mere 9 percent of pastoral roles in the evangelical church (even though women outnumber men in the pews across every denomination, in every age group).

Sharing my family's experience that year with my unbelieving friends felt like confirming all of their worst suspicions about church. I felt so discouraged in those conversations, wanting to share my pain with those I loved while also protecting the reputation of the church I'd wanted them to see differently for so long. "Well," I'd say, "this probably won't come as a surprise to you . . ."

Of course, I experienced this story as my mother's daughter—a limited, inherently biased vantage point. And while I was ashamed of the church's response, I was fiercely proud of my mom. From where I sat, I saw her most brilliant teaching unfold that year. Of course, there were many tears. But she showed me that my dignity and freedom aren't for the taking. She reminded me I have a voice. And I possess inner authority even when I don't have external power. She demonstrated that justice matters more than your legacy, and that sweeping evil—and the structures that protect it—under the rug will only leave more of a mess for those who inherit the house. I learned that there is a proper sequence to restoration work, that healing doesn't come before lament, and there can't be reconciliation without repentance. But most of all she helped me learn to stop saying "but."

If my mom could hold on to two truths at the same time, then I could learn to, no matter how contradictory they might seem. This is a story of pain *and* a story of triumph. Women were unsafe *and* they had opportunities to lead. Men and women can work together with mutual care to achieve great impact *and* things can go wrong. Someone can nurture others' spiritual growth *and* harm others. There is much at risk when men and women partner in ministry *and* there is much to gain.

My mom's inbox wasn't *only* full of people calling her the devil. There were messages of support too. And three little words that have never meant so much to us: *I believe you.*

Sometimes that is all people would say. And it was more than enough. People of certainty cling to only that which passes through the filter of their own experience. People of faith are students of the *both/and*, of death and resurrection, sin and redemption, loving their life enough to lose it. If it hadn't been my family in the spotlight, I sincerely wonder how quick I would have been to make room for an experience that would contradict my own. I had no choice but to move beyond my dualistic framework to accommodate Mom's story *and* all the good that I had witnessed at Willow. This event initiated a new chapter of doubt and deconstruction in my faith. As painful as this process has been, I would never trade it for the previous operating system built on simplicity and certitude. I suspect the church at large will need to grow more comfortable with complexity to survive the reckoning ahead.

Before I got to know Don and Terra, they had belonged to another church for forty years. Being at the same church for that many years sounds about as possible as staying at the same company for your whole career. A relic of generations past. Forty years! I haven't spent more than three years of my adult life in the same city. And yet when I think about what I want to believe about community, I admit I am intrigued by the bonds built through that kind of endurance. The connections formed, maintained, and strengthened over so many different seasons of life must be made of thick fiber, a stronger web. Which makes it all the more tragic when the net doesn't hold.

Terra knew well the fences that dictated where women could play, for she had explored every part of the yard available to her and tested the railing for weak spots. She led ministries but had to rely on men to make her announcements for her on Sundays. Boys could collect the offering, girls could count it. Women could appear on video but not live on stage. For Terra, an Eight on the Enneagram and a respected leader in her professional field, these limitations never aligned with what she understood of who God made her to be, who God was, and how to interpret Scripture. Yet she served faithfully in this church body for decades—developing a successful neighborhood small-groups program, supporting missions work, and using her social-work background to work with a committee on establishing a child safety policy. The latter project would be far more difficult than she anticipated.

The child safety committee consisted of two men, Terra, and another woman, Ada. The day they were called to defend their policy to the elders, Ada could not attend. Terra would be the only woman in the room.

A volunteer had blatantly overstepped the child safety guide-lines and defied warnings from the committee cautioning him against giving girls rides home and texting them throughout the day. The elders pushed back on the committee's decision to pro-hibit the man from serving, reflexively protecting the volunteer who they knew to be a respected, decent man in their community. Terra stood in front of a room full of male elders and male staff alongside the two other men on the committee. She was the only one with a background in social work. She and her committee members passionately argued that when it came to matters of child safety, no one deserved unearned trust and no one was exempt from adhering to the rules.

As she recounted this story, this is the part where Terra choked back tears, "Eventually, the other two men on our committee were nominated to become elders." Terra and Ada? They were barred from every other way they tried to contribute to the life of the church. Terra put together a proposal for a women's ministry, and the men in charge passed the project off to someone else. Ada offered to assist the youth ministry in training volunteers on how to handle difficult conversations—a skill she had developed through her role as a program director working with abused children—and she was denied that opportunity. The men were honored for their strength. The women were punished.

There are no awards for lady Lion Hearts.

Don and Terra left the church where they'd raised their family and served countless hours. Within only two years of attending a new church, Terra was nominated to join the board. Her relational intelligence, strategic thinking, and spiritual leadership are undeniable. I asked her how it feels now to be serving with her gifts, half-expecting an emotional outpouring of gratitude. She simply said, "Natural. It just feels like I get to be who I am."

Knowing Terra now I have a hard time imagining her cooped up and confined. I'm still trying to understand how she stayed in that environment as long as she did. Maybe wondering that is like asking my mom why she waited so long to say anything about the abuse of power she endured and witnessed. Research tells us this lag time is a result of multilayered social and psychological effects. *And* misogyny rooted in theology means that all too often women must choose between playing church wounded, with their hands tied behind their back, or not playing at all.

I also had enough "Girl Power" shirts in my closet to believe in the fence but never doubt that I could scale it. It's easy for me to forget that Mom and Terra inherited a different world from the one they fought to give me.

I've imagined a lot of apology scenes in my head. I've crafted rec-onciliation stories that would give the whole thing a Hallmark ending. Should Hollywood ever come calling, I'm ready to give the Willow story a punch-up. Unfortunately, though, healing is slow and unglamorous.

But a year into attending our tiny new church in Austin, an unexpected apology came. Our new pastor was not the perpe-trator, was not even a player in our story, but he recognized his complicity in an institution that had systematically excluded, si-lenced, and wounded women since its inception. And one weekend he chose to speak out about sexism and Christianity, a web our church is not yet free from.

Simply naming this knot won't detangle it. However, this un-earthing he initiated resulted in a *you had to be there* moment of great catharsis for our community—an experience that revealed to me the power of corporate lament. And it helped convince me to come forward with my gifts and trust this was an environment in which I might be welcome to lead and teach. I believe his words carry power on the page too. Perhaps they are words you need to hear. Maybe they are words you need to say.

Dear sweet sisters, mothers, daughters, grandmothers, wives:

Let me start by saying, "I'm sorry . . . truly."

I'm sorry for thinking of your emotions as untrustworthy and unwelcome in church leadership spaces.

I'm sorry for making fun of your many words, of your ability to spin a dozen plates simultaneously. What I should have said was, "I'm jealous at how your brain functions, given my inability to do more than one thing at a time."

I'm sorry for diminishing your tears, for overlooking your wise intuition, for ignoring your warnings when harm was on your radar, but not on mine, and for only half-listening while you unraveled your heart. This has a name, it's called ignorance. This is not what God dreamed of.

I'm sorry for allowing myself to be the center of your care and nurture while somehow neglecting to make you the center of mine.

I'm sorry for the years I was complicit in the thinking that said your beautiful and divine body is responsible for my own lack of control and inability to contain my hungry and undisciplined eyes; that's always been my work to do, not yours.

I'm sorry I thought open office doors and no-car-rides-alone with you was an act of courage and discipline on my part. This made you feel dangerous and shameful. This too has a name. It's called blame. This is not what God dreamed of.

I'm sorry the church I love has done as much, maybe more, to wound you as any other institution in society; we should have led, but we failed.

I'm sorry church still struggles to see you and to hear you, to understand you and to value your priceless contribution.

The truth is, you've led departments of ministry, in churches where I've served, without the title, authority, or the pay you deserved even though those same ministries would have failed without you.

I'm sorry that you've carried the local church on your back, on your volunteerism, on your ability to organize and execute—without the title. This has a name. It's called exploitation. This is not what God dreamed of.

I'm sorry for explaining what you literally just said, after you've finished, to men who could hear me but somehow couldn't hear you. I should have named that what that was—no matter what it cost me.

I'm sorry for actively dismissing your leadership, for passing you over for mentorship and promotion, and for being threatened by you when your ideas were way ahead of mine.

I'm sorry you grew up without a role model, someone who looked like you, leading from the center of power and authority, and influence; this has a name. It's called *fear*.

This is not what God dreamed of.

I'm sorry organized church hurt you by things it did and things it didn't do.

I'm sorry for remaining inactive and passive, unmoved and unmotivated when you were being injured by the same systems that assumed I was an expert, that assumed I had a voice and a right to use it, that assumed that my loud and persistent public rant was "prophetic and convicted," while it assumed that yours, when you used the exact same tone, when you said the very same things, was nagging and negative and emotionally disruptive.

But mostly I'm sorry that *we* made *you* feel ashamed of your gift, a beautiful and important gift we taught you to bury, because "the church wasn't ready to be led by a girl." Church, this too has a name. We call this *insecurity*.

And this, dear friends, is not what God dreamed of for the church.

So, sister, I'm sorry. We have to do better. And together we will.

—Jason Morriss

An apology is only the beginning. But it sure is a great place to start.

To be honest, my deepest sadness about what happened to my mom was the story I didn't get to tell about how the church responded. The story I wanted to tell my friends. So, here it is. My alternate ending:

> Well, this probably won't come as a surprise to you. Just like so many other institutions, the church is finally starting to reckon with its patriarchal roots and how sexism has silenced women, protected abusers, and kept women from bringing their gifts to bear, to the great loss of the community.
>
> My mom was actually at a church where she was given opportunities to lead and teach. That marked me as a young girl. I never questioned that my communication gifts were a mistake. And unfortunately, she was a victim of unchecked power.
>
> And when she and other women were brave enough to tell their story, the church was brave enough to hear it. And because the church wants to be like Jesus and because Jesus was a great champion and protector of women, they took serious steps to root out evil and the structures that protect it.
>
> They didn't add more rules that would make it harder for women to lead. They put systems in place for reporting abuse and seeking justice. And they kept asking women to lead. And they doubled down on the being-like-Jesus project. And everyone's had to learn that truth was never as simple as what your pastor told you or what Paul wrote on parchment. And that's been a sort of death.
>
> And something new is resurrecting. Women and men are figuring it out together. And it's hard. And it sucks that it's hard. And I'm really glad that the church sees that it's worth it.
>
> I think you'd like this place. Somehow, I still do.

6

The Mess We've Made

The Church's History of Exclusion and Oppression

NANCY

All people matter to God. This was one of our mantras at Willow Creek, decades before the Black Lives Matter movement. The very next sentence followed: *So they ought to matter to us.* We believed that truth to our core and sought to build a church community decorated with a warm and beautiful welcome mat for all people who might enter. Like the black rubber welcome mat outside my house's front door, this symbol of hospitality is intended to allow anyone, regardless of age, gender, race, profession, beliefs, values, appearance, disability, political leanings, language, sexual orientation, or background, to walk right in. Whether the church's front door is the Sunday-morning experience, a community service opportunity, a small group, or an online connection, the question is—what comes next? How far does our welcome extend? Once a person has crossed the threshold, can they access the other rooms, go deeper inside, or even sit at the table?

Perhaps no image more vividly describes God's community than the table. Luke 14 records the striking story of the great banquet—Jesus telling of a man who invited certain guests (I'm imagining prominent kinds of people, mayors or celebrities, who would make him look good) to his lavish banquet, only to be met with various lame excuses. The owner responds with anger, compelling his servant to go out into the streets and alleys, extending invitations to "the poor, the crippled, the lame, the blind."

When the table still wasn't full, even with those on the margins of society, the master told his servant to go out again and invite others so that the house will be bursting and every seat occupied. Church leaders these days are wrestling with this vital question: How long is your table? Who is truly included and invited to take a seat?

The vast majority of local churches in the United States and most other countries are filled with people who look like one another, who hold common beliefs, who share a specific worldview, who are similar. It's a cliché but still quite true that Sunday at 10:00 a.m. is the most segregated hour of the week in America. David W. Swanson, in his book *Rediscipling the White Church*, states that no more than 12 to 14 percent of American congregations are racially mixed.

I think we can agree that in the name of Jesus and his church, grave damage has been done historically to exclude various people groups from the table and invitations to the feast. We are divided all too often by race and also by political party, sexual orientation, and a wide array of socioeconomic and cultural differences. Too often our tables are filled with people who are *just like us*. In the past several years I find myself grieving over my complicit contribution to these divides.

In this chapter I will explore just two areas of exclusion and oppression in the local church that all of us must address if we have any hope of healing and thriving and becoming the kind of community God desires, creating tables like those we will surely experience together when we gather at the glorious ultimate banquet someday in eternity. Between now and then, we must face these two major reckonings (among others!)—the divide related to race and the divide related to sexuality. Let's start with race.

———

Just as each of us brings our own story to the question of the gender divide, the same is true of race. So here's a snapshot of my story. I am a White woman with Swedish, Scottish, and Welsh ancestry who was born on the south side of Chicago in an area called Englewood. Before I could walk, my parents joined the white flight to the suburbs, where I found myself walking among almost entirely White people. The only exceptions at my public school and in my church were a few Asian Americans and one girl with a Latin American heritage and a name I truly envied—*Marisa*.

All the rest of us looked the same. I think my first significant exposure to people of color happened when our grade school class, maybe around third grade, boarded a yellow bus and carried our brown paper lunch bags for a trip to the Field Museum in downtown Chicago. As we headed to the massive lunchroom in a long line of White children, we saw other long lines of brown- and black-skinned children also ready to eat. Filled with curiosity, I could not help staring at them, wondering about them, even feeling a little fearful of them. At the end of the day the White children got on their yellow buses to head back to the suburbs as the Black children boarded their yellow buses to the south or west side of the city, returning to our completely separate worlds.

In college at Southern Illinois University, three African American girls lived across the hall from me and made my experience much richer—Barbara, Candy, and Kathy, all from the same south side community of Chicago. Barbara and I clicked, and one summer I invited her to visit my family in the suburbs for a weekend. She didn't have an obvious way to travel to me, so my younger brother and I drove to her neighborhood to pick her up. This was in the days before GPS, and we got a little lost. Making our way up and down the streets of Roseland, large groups of young people hanging out on the corners, all with Black faces, stared at us wondering why we kept doing circles around the same block. I had no clear reason to feel unsafe, but even so I instructed my brother to lock the car doors. Eventually, we found Barbara, and she jumped in with her infectious smile and exuberance. Years later I'm more sensitive to what it must have felt like for her to be driven from the tiny brick bungalows and concrete apartment buildings out to the land with enormous yards of perfectly manicured green grass, into our White family's home, sitting at our table, knowing that she was likely the only person of color at that moment for miles around.

In the early years of Willow Creek our movie theater location was planted in an area whose demographics were well over 95 percent Caucasian. But as the years passed, more people of color moved into those suburbs, without our church reflecting much racial change. Our pastor and other leaders most definitely wanted to become a more diverse church, and we began focus groups with some of the rare non-White attenders in order to listen and figure out how. We learned that there is a huge difference between diversity and full inclusion. Diversity might make us feel better—like seeing people of color up on stage. Full inclusion is another matter entirely. Instead of expecting other cultures to simply adapt to our ways of worship and community building, true inclusion would mean that the White leaders would need to share our power and expand our preferences. So much harder!

Several years later in August 2014 I found myself at Soul City Church the first Sunday morning after the killing of Michael Brown in Ferguson, Missouri. As one of the first widely publicized police killings of Black people, that tragedy triggered protests and riots exposing again the vast racial divide in our country. Our pastors spoke into the moment and invited us all to get off our chairs, kneel, and join a few others sitting near us to pray for our country and our city. I joined with my husband and several people of color as we lamented and cried out to God for healing and unity. Soul City reflects the vast diversity of its location in the West Loop of Chicago. Every Sunday morning I look at the stage and around the room thinking it feels like the United Nations with so many different kinds of people—truly a taste of heaven. But inclusion is not without challenges. The week following our prayer moment on that August Sunday, our pastors received some angry emails from attenders who felt they did not pray enough for police officers and honor "the other perspective." We continue this journey of seeking to understand systemic racism, white supremacy, and what it means to sit at the table with one another.

Long after the events in Ferguson, I attended a Black Lives Matter rally in my sleepy, predominantly White suburb. I joined my voice calling out the names of others who experienced police brutality—Breonna Taylor, George Floyd, Ahmaud Arbery. Say their names! There was such power in shouting out the names in a large gathering of passionate people calling out for justice. Of course, simply attending a rally and shouting out names is only a prelude to what it would mean to work toward justice.

I would describe the last few years in my own life to be a reckoning regarding race. I am diving into books by minority authors who open me up to greater understanding. I believe our churches need to lament, grieve, and repair the sins of the past and the present that have oppressed people of color. Instead of rising with defensiveness, declaring, "I am *not* a racist!," my energy needs to focus on the truth that in a variety of ways I have been complicit in contributing to the racial divide. I carry unconscious bias (for example, when I locked my doors in Barbara's neighborhood). Those of us who happen to have been born with lighter skin find ourselves belonging to what writer Isabel Wilkerson calls "the dominant caste." White people in the United States benefit from countless privileges in a system erected to grant us advantages economically, socially, and politically.

Many churches are in the early stages of at least having the conversation. This work of listening and understanding is not a pretty walk on the beach. In her book *I'm Still Here*, church leader and writer Austin Channing Brown challenges me:

> Our only chance at dismantling racial injustice is being more curious about its origins than we are worried about our comfort. It's not comfortable conversation for any of us. It

is risky and messy. It is haunting work to recall the sins of our past. But is this not the work we have been called to anyway? Is this not the work of the Holy Spirit to illuminate truth and inspire transformation?

———

We grow in understanding as we listen to the stories.

I first encountered Elizabeth as a client for my coaching. She served as an executive for a major nonprofit organization. Born in Tanzania, Elizabeth came to the United States a few decades ago for education, eventually earning a PhD in cereal science and technology. She is the mother of a college-aged daughter and two sons in high school. Our coaching relationship has developed over time into a valued friendship. Elizabeth is helping me understand what it feels like for her to move within America—and her church—with dark skin.

Recently, Elizabeth returned to her home country for a few months, working from there while she attends to some family business for her mother. Our calls had to be carefully scheduled to accommodate time-zone differences. Not long ago Elizabeth was vulnerable with me about a discovery. She said that she realized after a few weeks in Tanzania that she felt incredibly relaxed. It wasn't just because she was home. The primary reason a burden lifted centered on the reality that in Tanzania, Elizabeth looks basically like everyone else. She is able to forget for long periods that she has dark skin. She can breathe. I noticed such a change in her spirit and countenance. Her shining eyes and beautiful smile radiated even through the Zoom call. She looked so happy.

When I asked her to tell me more, Elizabeth shared the story of an experience with her college-aged daughter, Imani, at a fabric store in the United States. My friend is a gifted quilter, and once a year she takes her high-quality sewing machine into the store for maintenance. As Elizabeth pushed her sewing machine in a box perched in the shopping cart, a young female employee approached and accused her of stealing the sewing machine. Immediately, Elizabeth says she went to a very submissive place, trying to explain that she already owned the machine. But when they walked later to the parking lot, anger set in. Elizabeth wanted to go back into the store and vent her frustration to the manager. Imani settled her mom down and talked her out of it. "Didn't you see that employee following us from the moment we went in? Mom, you are more oblivious to this kind of thing, but I grew up in this country, and I am followed in almost every store I enter. It's just our reality."

I have the privilege of walking around most places and not thinking about my skin color. I can breathe and relax and not worry about being accused of theft or being stopped in my car for no good reason. Sadly, Elizabeth tells me she has experienced bias against her even in her local church. In her predominantly White church Elizabeth has always felt like a visitor. More than once people have approached her thinking she might require financial assistance when she knows she is one of the primary donors there. Elizabeth was not visited when she was sick and does not feel seen by the leaders of her church. What would it look like if those of us in the majority would frequently sit with people of color and seek to understand?

In his book *Canoeing the Mountains,* Tod Bolsinger forecasts that sometime in the 2040s the United States will become a true ethnic plurality and urges the church to lead the way:

> As the dominant white culture in North America gives way to an increasingly pluralistic culture, imagine the impact that the church could have, imagine the witness the church could offer! In a world of fear marked by divisive group politics, imagine the difference the church could make.

Imagine that. We have an opportunity not only to behave like the Good Samaritan caring for the bruised and battered man. We must now also discuss the Jericho Road, the dangers along the way, and bolster its security. Let us, as brothers and sisters, join the forces of antiracism that boldly declare that in the kingdom of God, at the feast of the Lamb, all of us are treasured and welcome, and we will release our grip on power and privilege so that justice and unity are the hallmarks of our community. This work must be done. We cannot wait for heaven to see our tables include and also be led by people of all races who are children of God.

Even more stretching for many evangelical Christians than the question of race is whether our tables can make room for people in the LGBTQ+ community. This is the number one question I hear these days among church leaders. In his book *Unclobber*, Pastor Colby Martin writes,

> As it turns out, for many evangelical Christians "no discrimination" doesn't apply to gay people. . . . There is a unique brand of fear in many Christians when it comes to homosexuality. Filled with outlandish negative stereotypes about the gay community, and asinine horror stories about the "gay agenda," many conservative Christians freak out when it comes to our LGBTQ brothers and sisters.

Like most evangelical Christians, I was raised with an understanding that the Bible clearly condemns homosexuality as a sin. It wasn't even really a question on the table for the tribe I was a part of as we interpreted the Scriptures. In the 1980s, especially as the HIV/AIDS crisis swept through our nation and the globe, I saw many Christ-followers display compassion for the victims without condoning the behavior—our overly simplistic slogan was "Hate the Sin. Love the Sinner." That worked for a while . . . until it didn't. At least for me, I found my understandings shaken to the core mostly because of real people who crossed my path and softened my heart. Whenever we talk about the LGBTQ+ community, we must resist referring to it as an "issue" and remember we are talking about actual human beings and in many cases brothers and sisters in Christ. I will tell a few of their stories, beginning in the late 1970s in the earliest years of Willow Creek.

Rick's story. "I'm gay! I'm gay! I'm gay!" This was the anguished cry of our new church's drama writer as three of our pastors rushed to his hospital bed after he made a suicide attempt. I didn't learn of this tragedy until a few years later because I was away at college. Rick was one of the most gifted artists I have ever known—and I know a multitude of amazing artists. Quirky and somewhat socially awkward, with a lean and wiry body and curly blond hair, Rick displayed an intuitive sense of the human struggle as he wrote drama sketches for our Sunday morning services. Many weeks our attenders walked away from church remembering the drama more than anything else. As a part of his acting team I had no idea that Rick was gay. I now understand that he had not accepted that truth about himself either, not until a few years later. But Rick knew that he didn't fit somehow on staff at a church, and eventually he moved to downtown Chicago and never returned to church or, as I understand it, to his faith. Rick passed away of cancer in 2019.

Rachel's story. I do not know Rachel personally but have read her story along with other accounts of followers of Jesus who have a same-sex orientation and yet hold the traditional view of Scripture. Some of these believers have chosen the path of celibacy, seeking to honor God with their obedience and fighting the temptation to engage in same-sex relationships. Rachel's story took a different turn.

In her book *Born Again This Way*, Rachel describes how she discovered her attraction to women when she was in high school. Her family was not religious, and she felt free to experiment. While a student at Yale University, Rachel began a search that led her to a relationship with Jesus. Her devotion to Christ deepened as she found support and friendship in a Christian community on campus. Through several twists and turns and careful study of the Scriptures, Rachel became convinced that living out her same-sex attraction would not be God's best for her and would actually be disobedient. She assumed that her only option would be a life of celibacy. In her own words:

> To choose celibacy, Jesus must be really precious to you. What a chance to testify that he is! You only give up something awesome for something even better. I could only give up the pleasures of a girlfriend—even someday a wife—for the more pleasurable embrace of Christ.

Plot twist—in 2007, Rachel married a man named Andrew. They became friends on a summer missions project, and at first it never occurred to Rachel to be interested in Andrew romantically. She does not believe that heterosexual marriage can make a person straight and writes that marriage is not promised or the best option for all humans. And yet over time Rachel felt her heart opening up to Andrew and began to trust that she had enough attraction to make it work. She says she entered into marriage with clarity and freedom and that marriage "will be where God leads some of his people, perhaps unexpectedly." Andrew and Rachel are now raising a young daughter together.

Rachel's story makes me wonder how we might always make room in this conversation for God's abundant love and provision to surprise us.

David's story. David served as the senior pastor of a Baptist church in a mid-size Southern city. One day his fourteen-year-old son Tim asked his parents if they could talk in private about something. So they took him into a room, shut the door, and with no hesitation Tim said, "I think I'm gay." David says he felt the air go out of the room. He asked Tim how he knew, hoping that maybe he was experiencing some confusion. David also admits to panicking, filled with anxiety about what this discovery could mean to him professionally as the senior pastor of a conservative congregation.

David and his wife, Joanie, have walked through many stages with their son. At first they took him to a Christian counselor who was empathetic but not willing to endorse homosexuality. Graciously but firmly the counselor conveyed to Tim that his only viable options were to either find a way to make a straight relationship work or remain celibate. So Tim dated a series of girls in high school and then in college, only to have those relationships eventually fizzle. When he enrolled in Princeton Seminary, Tim told his parents it was time for him to be open about his sexual orientation, that he could no longer try to change. Tim expressed the deep desire to someday be in a monogamous, faithful relationship.

Meanwhile, David was on his own journey. He thought it would be hypocritical for him to abandon his traditional view of what he believed Scripture taught just out of love for his son. And so he studied. And pondered. And explored. David read several books, including *A Letter to My Congregation* by Ken Wilson. Tim was very kind and patient with his parents as they dialogued about sexuality and Scripture. While Tim began dating men, David eventually resigned as pastor to work for a nonprofit Christian organization. David's process of theological reflection combined with prayerful listening to the Spirit over several years has led him to a place where he can affirm same-sex orientation and gay marriage while still holding a high view of Scripture.

David counts it a tremendous privilege to have been invited to participate in Tim's ordination ceremony, with Tim now serving as a Presbyterian pastor. Tim married Perry, and together they have adopted a little boy named James. For David and Joanie the wedding was a profound experience of the presence of God, celebrating a covenantal commitment.

David and Tim's story causes me to wonder what kept Tim in the faith and how both father and son found a way for Christianity to be at the center of their lives in the midst of their discernment.

If you're at all like me, you struggle to understand how people who authentically love Jesus and walk with God can come to remarkably different positions on the question of homosexuality and gay marriage. What are we to believe? I know I am not alone as an evangelical Christian wresting with this divide between my head and my heart. These questions are agonizing, especially for those of us who know and love people who are gay.

So what is the path forward? I think we must begin with humility and openness. Jesus modeled for us throughout his ministry a passionate love for those on the margins, for the outcasts. The religious leaders slammed Jesus for hanging out with the riffraff. Surely, if Jesus walked among us today, he would move toward the LGBTQ+ community, not shunning them.

I also call us to openness to our interpretation and understanding of the Scriptures. I challenge those of us who have held the traditional view to dig into scholarship from a variety of theologians and pastors across the spectrum. As I do my study I wish I could find a slam dunk, irrefutable interpretation. That has not been my experience so far. But what if all of us, no matter our position on this question, adopt a spirit of curiosity, examining our views to make room for the Spirit to guide us?

As Christian leaders and pastors all over the globe wrestle with these vital questions, how unifying would it be if we could choose to believe the best about one another, even those who hold a view different from the one we hold? And what if we stopped using a person's view on homosexuality as the ultimate litmus test for being at the table, contributing to the deepening divisiveness among followers of Jesus? Let us remember that God's unconditional love is available to all of his children, no matter where we land on these questions.

I do know this. We cannot run away and hide from these questions about sexuality. We also cannot be silent, hoping that gay people will feel welcome even if we are not clear about whether they can ever be a member at our church, serve at our church, dedicate or baptize children at our church, be married at our church, or one day aspire to leadership or even full-time ministry at our church. The very least we can offer is clarity.

I simply urge all followers of Jesus to hold our point of view loosely, to do the deep study, and no matter where we land, to frequently utter these vitally important words: *I could be wrong*.

———

I think about my old friend Rick and grieve that he never felt welcome or even safe enough to confess his truth. Back in the 1970s Rick could not have imagined a church might exist where he could flourish and grow and not abandon his identity as a gay man.

Every church must take a truthful look at how long our tables are, at what our welcome mats mean. Where we have wounded others because of racial differences or sexuality or any other reason, we must lament, confess, and repair, building bridges across these divides in the name of Jesus. I have hope for the future of the local church if we will do this kind of fundamental, God-honoring work. And I look to my daughter and cowriter Samantha, with respect and support, as she found her way to a church much different from the one I was raised in.

SAMANTHA

Will and I get pizza on a Sunday after church. We're at the stage of our relationship where we suspect we might be together forever, but we're still sizing up a few things. We are test driving the car. We go slowly, with caution. But sometimes something bursts out—one of us slams on the brakes or accelerates unexpectedly as if to make sure this vehicle can handle it, can keep us safe together while keeping each of us whole.

"I think the church has done more harm than good," Will blurts out. He takes a bite of pizza, eyes darting up to see if he's gone too far.

We'd been attending church together for some time now. Will loved talking about Jesus and wanted to follow his teaching. He often talked about how the message of the gospel had the power to liberate and encourage so many of his friends who were in search of greater meaning for their lives. But church kept getting in the way for him. Sometimes our postservice debrief would make me feel like we had just experienced two completely different events. I was still moved by a meaningful worship experience, and Will would ask about the chorus that said God was "the name above all names." "Why are Christians so obsessed with declaring the superiority of their God?" I was inspired by baptism Sunday. "That felt manipulative," he'd say. "Why did they keep saying there were some of us who needed to jump out of our seats and get up there? Shouldn't you make that decision more carefully?"

After a message about Jesus calling us to love everyone and all being welcome, Will sensed there were limits. Did that include our queer friends? Or were they only welcome if they were willing to change? (And were you ever really *welcome* if there is an expectation you become someone else eventually?) I was ready to dish out more money for the new building campaign, and Will asked what was wrong with the old one. His questions were, frankly, exhausting. But they were penetrating. They reached a part of me buried underneath rote answers and unearned trust. He was inviting (urging) me to see the institution I was born into as it appeared from the outside. I wasn't ready.

I put down my pizza. I needed both hands for my dramatic rebuttal. I'd had a front-row seat to the good the church had wrought! He just hadn't seen it. I began my monologue by painting a picture for this confused and inexperienced boyfriend of mine. With tenderness I told him of a gymnasium full of meals and seeds for families in Zambia. I pulled in the cars program that restored and provided cars to single moms. I mentioned ministries for those who are grieving or in recovery—and that was just one church in the suburbs!

I skillfully began my crescendo. Who's down at the border getting bus tickets for immigrants? Catholics. Who helped give rise to hospitals? Churches. Orphanages? Starts with a *C*. And schools? I made the sign of the cross. How about Christian abolitionists? Also Martin Luther King Jr.! Mother Teresa! Sojourner Truth! I was just shouting names now. Our waiter came and left. Not to mention any of the quiet, sacrificial acts of service committed by people who have been transformed by the teachings of the local church! Net positive! I'm sure of it! I sat back. A little sweaty. But pleased with my persuasive performance.

Will was unconvinced. *What was it he saw?* I wondered. As I sat in the aftermath of my hasty defense, questions from deep within began to surface. They transported me to memories I'd discarded, unsure where to file them.

I am no longer at the restaurant eating pizza. I am studying abroad in Ghana. I'm visiting the Cape Coast Castle, the port through which untold numbers of slaves were imprisoned until they departed for America and the Caribbean. I walk through the archway to the Portuguese chapel where the slaveholders worshiped, and above the door engraved in stone is a reference to Psalm 132. I am told it means that "this is where God lives."

I am seventeen. My homecoming date comes out to me. I don't know how to react; we didn't cover this in youth group. Vaguely, I remember I'm supposed to love him and also hate this part of him? I don't know what to say.

I am at Will's apartment and he's on the phone with his mom. Knowing faith is a big part of his son's girlfriend's life, she's just given church another try, after twenty-five years of sporadic attendance. She tells him she picked a church in Denver and just showed up. Within the first ten minutes they were talking about sex—who can have it, who they can have it with, and when. She leaves. Never mind, then. If this is all this is about.

I am on vacation in Machu Picchu. Our tour guide tells us of the Incan temple Corichancha and how the Spanish built their church on top of its ruins. He says this was commonly practiced throughout the Americas as native religions were destroyed and subsumed into the Christianity of conquest.

"I guess you can't really measure it, either way," I say to Will quietly. We ask for the check.

———

I was aware as a child that Willow was a seeker-friendly church. (I wondered what the seeker-hostile churches were like!) And as an adult I attended other large, evangelical churches with an aggressive focus on new people. For a church regular, Christmas and Easter services began to feel like going back to kindergarten for a day. I would hear the ABC (admit, believe, choose) salvation prayer prayed *over* and *over* as if the pastor was speaking to someone hard of hearing or trying to transcend a language barrier.

There seems to be an assumption that new people in church simply don't know much of anything about the whole Jesus project. They are a blank slate. Their primary barrier to accepting and living in the love of Jesus is that they have never been offered the invitation before. But new guests in a church are not new to the church. Whether they've attended elsewhere or not, their mind is full of impressions: Christians they've met, history books, billboards, protests, and news stories that have formed opinions, fears, suspicions, and questions. The church is embedded in almost every aspect of American life. It shows up in politics and classrooms, in weddings and funerals. God is in our Pledge of Allegiance and on the dollar bill. You cannot escape its influence. No one is new to church.

Oh, how I wish they were, though! How I long for a chance for the church to start over. We are like the youngest of a bunch of trouble-making siblings walking into high school determined to make a name for herself, to be independent and well-liked and a good student. But we are someone's sister before we ever get to be someone new, defined by those who share the same name and got here first.

Will tried out a few churches in his first year alone in Austin. When I came down to visit and wanted to check out the no-Easter-service place, he said, "Okay. But you can't tell anyone it's our first time. Don't sign anything. Don't talk to anyone. Let's just sit quietly in the back." Will had felt a little bit, um, *hounded* as a first-timer at the churches he'd visited without me.

I obeyed Will's rules, and we took seats near the back. The teaching was on Matthew 5 and how Jesus challenges our categories of who is included. The pastor invited us to consider our own racism, sexism, and homophobia as well as the evangelical church's passion for deciding who gets to be loved and who doesn't. He interrogated the American church's love affair with nationalism, capitalism, and political might.

So often I went to church and was convicted to look within. I couldn't remember ever being invited to consider the larger systems I was a part of and how my participation in those institutions perpetrated evil. And I don't know if I had *ever* heard a church critique the church. For Will this was an olive branch. He felt that because this community was comfortable enough to name (and see!) the damage the evangelical church had wrought—especially to people of marginalized identities—then at least he wouldn't feel crazy here. Maybe, just maybe, a church that could critique itself would be a church he could trust. As soon as the service ended he approached the pastor and said, "Where do we sign up? Can you send us emails? What's the next step?" I was shocked. So much for slipping in and out!

In the eyes of some seekers, predominantly White churches are inextricably linked to an ancient institution with a legacy of conquest and a lust for power that has oppressed those at the margins. We know that such treatment of any human being grieves the heart of God, who imbued every single one of us with his divine image. The good news (if we can see it as such) is that we get to participate in restoration. That cycle of injustice stops when a community of faith is brave enough to name it, lament, repent, learn, listen, repair, and maybe even, as author and activist Adrienne Maree Brown writes, "move at the speed of trust" to pursue reconciliation. I believe the most defining characteristic of a truly incarnational church in the future is that it will be a church reckoning with its past. In particular, churches must face how we have failed to follow Jesus in liberating people at the margins of our society, those who fall outside the White, straight, affluent, physically normative center where I have had the privilege of camping out for my entire life.

The particularities of the wounds the church has inflicted on Black people, the LGBTQ+ community, Indigenous brothers and sisters, people with disabilities, and people experiencing poverty matter. And it is outside the scope of this book to consider a nuanced approach for repairing the harm done to each of these communities, in part because we must listen to, believe, and follow the lead of members of those populations we've hurt. Each of these topics could be its own book. But I believe there is a posture that will serve a church that seeks to repair—a posture defined by humility, repentance, and a willingness to listen, be led, and take sacrificial action. That is what I urgently and enthusiastically invite us to consider. For the sake of the church. For the sake of the oppressed. And for the sake of our hearts.

I too am on this journey of reckoning, and I long for the church to lead me deeper into this sacred work. I suspect that the more I undo and uncover and unlearn all that my unearned position has taught me, the more I will see of Jesus: the brown-skinned criminal enemy of the state, born to a poor woman caught up in a sex scandal; the man who always moved toward those for whom life was not easy, and in doing so, demonstrated the path of freedom and grace available to the Pharisee and the rich young ruler too. As Lisa Sharon Harper writes in *The Very Good Gospel*, "If one's gospel falls mute when facing people who need good news the most—the impoverished, the oppressed and the broken— then it's no gospel at all."

———

I see the church's heart for racial reconciliation and understand why we are in a hurry to get there. My friend Noemi has helped me see the ignorance behind our haste. Noemi is led by a deep curiosity and the openmindedness of a true mystic. She asks the kind of questions that can change the temperature of a room. This happened in one small group in which we were bemoaning the lack of diversity at our church. Noemi, the only woman of color in our group, pointed to the assumption underlying this conversation that people *want* to be in White spaces.

I see this in myself—a longing for the appearance of diversity without an appetite for the work of repair and justice.

As a Black and Dominican lesbian, Noemi has run into many of the walls the American church has constructed. She told me, "Certainly, the church needs to reckon with race. With LGBTQ+ stuff. But lately I'm thinking about the lament we never had for all of those early Indigenous peoples and their faith that we eliminated. We can never get that back. We can't build bridges with the Black church or the Latino church until we see those things." Noemi wants to see the church work backward before rushing forward.

Our churches are built on top of ruins. Why did I have to go to Peru to learn that? What if that was something the church was brave enough to teach me?

For as much as we love telling old stories in church, there is a whole lot of history we seem determined to avoid. I have attended church most Sundays of my life. Let's say I went 80 percent of the time. Maybe 3 percent of the time my sister and I were doing cartwheels in the lobby and 2 percent of Sundays I was too distracted by a hot drummer to pay attention. That's still 1,248 Sundays. I've gone to church in all six cities I've lived in. I've heard great sermons on Martin Luther King Jr. weekend and many calls for racial reconciliation. I've heard many adaptations of the Good Samaritan and recited Galatians 3:28 as a promise of heaven marked by unity. But in 1,248 services I never heard the story of how the White American church compromised with slavery and racism. Jemar Tisby told me that story in his book *The Color of Compromise*.

What if the church were courageous enough to tell the truth about itself? If we removed the log from our own eye, what would we be able to see? Could we see the image of God in those we've stripped of their humanity? I think we'd see God's face in people like Rob.

Rob is a brilliant actor and educator. We taught together at a theater-training program for young people. I saw so many kids who wanted to become Rob. And Rob did all he could to help them become *them*. Everyone shines brighter in Rob's presence. And from his first moments on earth, Rob was told he belonged to God.

As the child of a pastor he jokes that his oft-repeated origin story is a lot of pressure to live up to. Moments after he was born, Rob's dad laid hands on him and said, "Father God, we give this child back to you!" Rob's parents told him he was a prophet. A good and perfect gift. "So," Rob says through tears, "I've never questioned that I was born with a purpose. And now I realize that purpose is that I might be the last project my dad—and the church—needs to work on."

A gay man growing up in Iowa, Rob went on to endure a great deal of trauma in Christian spaces. He came of age during the AIDS crisis and remembers hearing church members weaponize the virus as God's punishment on those who loved as Rob did. His college ministry staff and peers laid hands on him and tried to "pray away the gay" as Rob tried to remember who he was: a good and perfect gift. A prophet. A man with a purpose.

———

The week that the "Nashville Statement" was released, Houston was underwater and the nation was reeling from a white supremacist rally in Charlottesville, Virginia. This multiauthored document with many noteworthy signatories makes a biblical defense of traditional views relating to gender and sexuality. My social media newsfeed that week was a blur of unequal and unsettling news, as it so often is. But the contrast offered a stark depiction of the choices that lie before all churches. Some decried the racism on display in Charlottesville. Many had their hands dirty, serving and showing up for those affected by the floods. And some were proudly sharing the Nashville Statement. This image haunts me still: 150 pastors cloistered in some hotel conference room fine-tuning who is and isn't a good and perfect gift while their neighbors are gasping for air.

There were many rebuttals written in response to the Nashville Statement, including the "Nazareth Statement," written by the Rev. Jacqueline J. Lewis. She wrote,

We believe that Jesus of Nazareth's most profound teaching was in response to the question of which commandment is the greatest. Jesus said to love God with everything we have—our whole soul, mind, heart and strength, and to love our neighbor as we love ourself.

We believe that Jesus' love was revolutionary love. . . .

We believe that in every age the Church will have to wrestle with what it means to be faithful today. This is what it means to be disciples. Ours is a living faith; God is still speaking.

Do we believe that God is still speaking? Allowing myself to ask critical questions of the church has been an adventure in release. It's startling to discover that some of what I had learned from this institution merits interrogation. If they perpetuated harm, then maybe so did I. Perhaps our intent did not always match our impact. As challenging and sometimes painful as this new understanding has been, I feel God's presence in all of it, even if the old wineskins will no longer do.

Richard Rohr writes, "People inside the status quo usually have much to lose. They don't necessarily have ill will; it's just that they're living in the only world they've ever imagined."

———

I got to watch my mom reimagine. After more than fifty years of following Jesus, she could have considered herself a fully evolved expert on faith in the modern age. Transformation complete. Salvation secured. But she was brave enough to say, "I don't know. I might be wrong." And eventually the question that can change everything is "What if?" I've watched how this shift toward deeper curiosity and compassion for the LGBTQ+ community has opened up new possibilities in her heart and her partnerships with pastors and churches.

On this particular issue I can be impatient. Many of my friends are too. Marriage equality passed when I was twenty-five. As a high school teacher, Will is already warning me we'll be tested by Gen Z, who is far more concerned for those at the margins than we ever were at their age. I can't predict what the hot-button theological topic will be in my second half of life or who I'll be challenged to love. But surely the relentless river of compounding revelation will bring me to a moment when I have the choice to dam the flow or follow the Spirit of liberation. I hope I possess the courage of my mom and others of her generation to question the unquestionable. I hope I listen to those whom my opinion deeply impacts. And ultimately I hope I err on the side of love and freedom. The bad news is I am terrible at saying I'm wrong. My apologies are of the "I'm sorry *you* had a pen in your pockets when I put those pants in the wash" or "Huh. I'm sorry you felt that way" variety. I will need to be attending a "What if?" church to be discipled in the art of repenting, which, it turns out, actually means "changing your mind."

And that must be the beginning, not the end. Repair won't take place in our minds any more than we can think our house clean or debate a new plant into blooming. On the matter of racial reconciliation, Austin Channing Brown writes in *I'm Still Here*,

A great many people believe that reconciliation boils down to dialogue: a conference on race, a lecture, a moving sermon about the diversity we'll see in heaven. But dialogue is productive toward reconciliation only when it leads to action—when it inverts power and pursues justice for those who are most marginalized. Unfortunately, most "reconciliation conversations" spend most of their time teaching white people about racism. In too many churches and organizations, listening to the hurt and pain of people of color is the end of the road, rather than the beginning.

There is a dialogue spin cycle in the LGBTQ+ conversation as well. Some churches get stuck in "discernment" for years on end. Education matters, but as we read and tinker and debate and meet and process and reflect and listen, precious human beings are working, hurting, falling in love, and raising kids in the world our intolerance has built.

I regret that I was content for too long to be a part of churches where there was not full inclusion. The issue affected me in theory, but not in practice. I ignored the pit in my stomach in part because I hadn't seen an unabashedly affirming church yet. I thought being "in discernment" about it was pretty rare! I failed to imagine something better.

We are told that when one member of the body suffers, we all suffer. If this is true, the church has been sick for a long time. Maybe the pit in our stomach when the church fails to stand up for the oppressed is a holy link connecting us to the part of the body that suffers. Do we believe that our salvation is inherently linked?

———

There were times when Rob strayed from the church that had hurt him. But he felt the persistent nudging of a loving presence behind him, sometimes quite literally. Rob was in a production of

Angels in America in Chicago. The image they chose for the poster was an angel peering over his shoulder, pressing a book toward his heart. Every night they would reach that moment in the show, and the angel character would speak her line in Rob's ear, "You can't outrun your occupation. You know me, prophet."

And so Rob is back in church. While he could be in relationship with the angel on his shoulder without participating in the institution that has wounded him, he would tell you, "We need each other." I hope tomorrow's church won't let anything get in the way of that gospel truth. Not comfort, not metrics, not donors, not pride, and not fear.

The extent of our damage is grim, but I have hope for the church of tomorrow. I have hope for the church that owns the self-harm we've inflicted on members of our own body. I have hope for the antiracist church. And I have hope for the affirming church.

After Will signed us up for emails, we kept going back to that little Texas chapel. This church doesn't just welcome LGBTQ+ people but *wants* their full inclusion and participation. After three years of attending, I could never go back to anything less. It would be like choosing to watch TV in black and white after you've seen what it looks like in color.

In the past when I would invite friends to church with me, I used to worry whether or not it would be a "good" weekend. In the years when my mom was on staff, I could usually get the scoop about the content. (Was the weekend all about giving toward the latest capital campaign? Was it about sex? Hell?) I've sweated through many services next to a guest I didn't want to scare away. Maybe you know this feeling. Maybe you've been the guest.

After a few months of attending our new and imperfect church, I realized that for the first time I was sitting in a place where I wouldn't hesitate to invite *anyone* on *any weekend*. Not because our church was a pure, incarnational vision of God's kingdom on earth. Far from it.

I could invite friends without fear because I didn't feel as if I were hiding anything. Queer people wouldn't hear they were welcome and be met with invisible fences once they got more involved. This community has a long way to go on equity and representation, *and* they were interrogating how the church has contributed to white supremacy in America and inviting us into the sacred work of confession, lament, and repair. Not just one weekend a year. This invitation to move toward the margins was consistently being made—surfacing throughout Scripture when you're looking for it—like putting a new lens on the camera. *This church was unabashedly not there yet.* And this humility made Will and me feel at home. For we are works in progress too.

With astonishing charity Rob says this sustained effort is his simple prayer for the church. He compares it to a conversation with a Black friend in which he was working too hard to demonstrate his allyship. She said to him, "I don't need you to be cured of racism right now. I need you to act like someone who's taking a good look in the mirror, who sees himself clearly—imperfections and all—and says, 'You know what, I'm working on it.'" This captured his feelings toward the church as it addresses LGBTQ+ trauma. "I'd just like them to be working on it. They don't need to be cured yet."

Noemi too displays remarkable patience toward the church of her childhood. They loved her family well through great loss. While they aren't yet wholly affirming, "They aren't in a bubble," she says. "They at least see me. And my humanity. They are grappling with it."

I can't quite fathom this level of grace and patience from those who've endured such suffering at the hands of the present and the historical church. How can they still believe in redemption? Will they tire of offering forgiveness? What is this strength they possess? To me, it looks a lot like Jesus.

7

Behind the Curtain

Creating a Healthy Culture

NANCY

As we come to this last chapter, I carry a deep concern that our readers will find our tone so far to be too critical and angry about the church. Anger is not a comfortable emotion for me; I grew up thinking it was not Christian to ever be angry or, worse, express anger. When I think about my Savior, Jesus, the first word that comes to mind is simply *love*. And yet the Gospels reveal moments when Jesus raged with anger. The most obvious example of a truly stirred-up Jesus took place when he saw the outrageous greed, dishonesty, and self-interest of the merchants who converted a house of worship into a strip mall. Jesus stormed into the temple crafting a whip out of ropes and drove out the currency exchange along with the sheep and cattle, tossing their coins and overturning their booths selling merchandise to the worshipers flooding to Jerusalem for Passover. I imagine the taut muscles on Jesus' face and his strong arms as he exploded with anger. The disciples rarely saw this dimension of their teacher, and John tells us they remembered a prophecy from the Psalms:

> For zeal for your house consumes me,
> and the insults of those who insult you fall on me.
> (Psalm 69:9)

I believe there is a place for zealous anger about ways the church is not what it should be. Some followers of Jesus are not only angry but also in pain because of the church. Our pain and anger are integrated, one often triggering the other. My former pastor used to say, "There's nothing like the church when the church is working right." I could not agree more. But sadly there's also nothing like the church when it isn't working right. And there's nothing quite like church pain.

Church pain is nothing new. It goes back to the earliest church when the apostle Paul and Barnabas debated and damaged their relationship over the role they thought should be played by Mark. Down through the centuries well-known leaders like George Whitefield from Britain, Saint Patrick of Ireland, and Jonathan Edwards of America experienced deep church pain inflicted by other Christians. A study from George Barna that goes back a few years now revealed that nearly four out of ten unchurched people avoid church because of a bad experience in church. Even though most of us know better, we tend to be surprised by church pain because we expect so much more from followers of Jesus.

A typical American response is to simply quit the church. Many former church people decide, *From now on it's just going to be Jesus and me. I give up on the people of God and this institution called the church.* Far more Americans would say they believe in God than those who belong to a house of worship. For the first time since the late 1930s, fewer than half of Americans say they belong to a church, synagogue, or mosque, according to a recent Gallup report. The rise of the Nones is up to 21 percent, with some pollsters placing the figure at 30 percent.

Many of us are wired to be lone rangers in our spiritual lives. The pandemic that began in late 2019 fueled that sense of being on our own, getting our teaching online at home in our pajamas. Yet I don't believe isolation is a viable option for a true follower of Jesus. I've read that Jesus has a thing for the church, which he called his bride. We cannot say we love God and not love his people. And if God's primary agenda is to transform us to become more and more like Jesus in our everyday life, that transformation happens most powerfully in the context of community. Rachel Held Evans, in her powerful book *Searching for Sunday*, wrote, "Christianity isn't meant to simply be believed; it's meant to be lived, shared, eaten, spoken and enacted in the presence of other people. They remind me that, try as I may, I can't be a Christian on my own. I need a community. I need the church."

How fervent is your zeal for the church these days? I am grateful to say that while my zeal meter rises and falls, currently it burns intensely—mostly because I do not see another viable alternative. I'm convinced that the local church truly is God's plan A for bringing people home to him. I want to be a participant in beautifying the bride of Christ, doing whatever I can in my small corner of the universe to create a healthier, more loving, more holy community of faith.

I have a friend who experienced deep pain at a church and ended up needing to leave it for the sake of her soul. A few years later she was a part of a different church, and I inquired how it was going for her and whether she had come to know any of the pastors and staff. Her response could make me laugh or cry. She said, "I don't want to get to know them. I'd rather live with my fantasy that all is well up at the top than risk finding out there is any kind of trouble."

——

As I coach church leaders, I hold what I believe is a realistic view (hopefully not a cynical one) that every church is dysfunctional in some way. It's a question of degree. This is because all people in the church are sinners, and we show up with our redeemed and healthy traits along with our shadow, sinful side. My fervent hope is that the closer we go to the center of any church, to its leadership core, the more love and Christlike character we will discover.

Every church creates a culture. A culture is essentially the way of life of a group of people, including their behaviors, beliefs, and values. My simple way of defining culture is how it feels to be there. The leaders of any church greatly influence the creation of its culture. Healthy teams and cultures are built by healthy leaders. Toxic cultures are devised by toxic leaders. But every individual in the church also plays a part in either reinforcing or seeking to bring change to the culture.

I am learning that the most difficult person to lead is myself, and my energy must focus on my transformation to Christlikeness before I even consider challenging someone else. This truth was beautifully captured by Etty Hillesum, a young Jewish woman who was killed at Auschwitz. From her journals we read of a conversation with her friend Klaas about the hatred and bullying she saw within her community. Look how she turns the lens around for a selfie on her character, writing in her diaries, *An Interrupted Life*: "It is the only thing we can do, Klaas, I see no alternative, each of us must turn inward and destroy in himself all that he thinks he ought to destroy in others. And remember that every atom of hate we add to this world makes it still more inhospitable."

As I have turned inward more intently in the past several years, I see how readily I want to call out pride or abuse of power in others without focusing on my capacity for the very same sins. I played a role as a senior leader in a highly influential and visible church. Now I can see how those roles, and in particular the pulpit, can be breeding grounds for toxic behavior.

A few years ago I seized the opportunity to participate in a small-group leadership cohort with Jim Dethmer, an executive coach who once served as a pastor. I spent a year meeting with a group of ten executives, as one of the only faith leaders in the group. Together we aimed to grow in our conscious leadership skills, to speak truth to ourselves and one another. At one of our meetings Jim went up to a flipchart and drew a cycle he has observed among corporate leaders. Almost immediately I realized how much this cycle pertains to those of us in the church. I invite you to look at this cycle through the lens of your own life.

The cycle begins with *obligation*. Anyone in a key leadership role carries enormous obligations. For a senior pastor there are countless sermons to write, a staff to be led, strategies to discern, vision to cast, people to care for, facilities to be fixed or built, money to be raised. There are not enough hours in the day, and all of these obligations often trigger stress. Leadership can also be extremely lonely.

The next step in the cycle is *resentment*. How easy it is for the leader to feel resentful, at first in small ways, about all this obligation! We can begin to think that no one understands how hard the job is, that we aren't receiving adequate pay or recognition for all we carry, that there is no margin whatsoever to do what we might *want* to do instead of what we *have* to do. We think we have no choice. Casting ourselves in the role of a victim sneaks in over time and can lead to the next phase of the cycle.

Obligation and resentment can lead to *entitlement*. The leader begins to believe that because of all this obligation, they deserve something and can be considered an exception to the rules or even to Scripture in some area. Andy Crouch writes about how we create celebrity cultures in our churches that prop up our leaders as "other than." We start to believe we are as special as everyone else thinks we are. We have a right to something.

Entitlement can then lead to *escape*. The pastor or leader begins to cherish the idea that they are entitled to some area of escape. This could be numbing with video games, gambling, pornography, alcohol or substance abuse, gluttony, or engaging in an affair. Often the leader compartmentalizes this behavior into one tiny corner of life, justifying that it is deserved in some way to make up for all the obligation. But this escape—especially for those who follow Jesus—carries with it guilt and shame. The guilt can propel the leader back to fulfilling even more obligations, to working even harder at ministry, and the cycle continues.

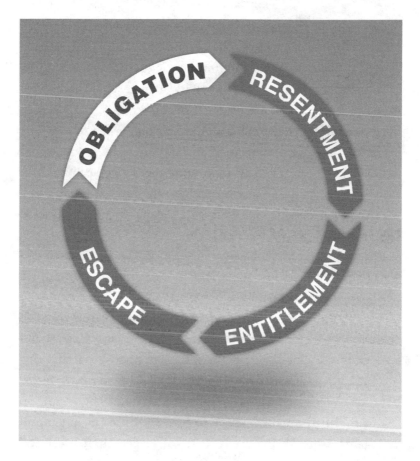

Learning about this cycle has been hugely helpful to me, both in understanding my capacity for thinking I'm entitled as well as giving me greater empathy for the challenges of other senior leaders. The good news is that the cycle is not inevitable. It can be disrupted if we choose. But first, another word about celebrity cultures within the church.

———

Diane Langberg is a highly respected psychologist who specializes in working with victims of clergy abuse. In many of her teachings Diane describes the culture that can be created by powerful, dynamic leaders who are treated like celebrities whether they serve a congregation of one hundred or ten thousand. Almost always, these leaders form an inner circle of other leaders. I was once a part of an inner circle like that. Diane teaches that people in the inner circle can be complicit in some way of propping up the powerful leader and helping to enable him or her to continue his or her behavior of narcissism in a culture of fear. Why would any of us be complicit? Why do we sometimes give up our efforts to speak truth and call out sin? At least in part it is because the inner-circle leaders benefit from what Diane calls the "refracted light" of that powerful leader. Ouch.

Whenever a prominent leader falls, those of us who surrounded or supported that leader must look at ourselves to see what we need to own, what we need to confess. I am examining why I did not speak up more often, why I joined others in somehow accepting what should not have been accepted. While I was in senior leadership at Willow, I did not know the extent of sexual sin going on. But I did see abuse of power. I had something to gain in terms of my own platform and area of ministry in the arts by staying on the team. I had my own power to protect. I now deeply regret giving up too quickly in my efforts to call leadership to account. I cared too much for my own comfort, approval, and opportunity. And I was also simply too afraid. If you find yourself concerned about anything in your church that seems broken or off, practice what we hear all the time at the airport—"If you see something, say something." Every person in a community of faith is responsible to help create the healthiest, most God-honoring culture possible. It will never be perfect. But it can be good.

Authors Scot McKnight and Laura Barringer paint a picture of a healthy church in their book *A Church Called Tov: Forming a Goodness Culture That Resists Abuses of Power and Promotes Healing.* *Tov* is from the Hebrew word for *good.* I love the vision they cast:

In the circle of *Tov*, when we practice the habits of empathy and compassion, extending grace, putting people first, telling the truth, promoting justice, and serving others, tov emerges in the culture and we all become more like Christ. Goodness becomes an agent that influences every aspect of our lives.

When my work as a coach brings me to a variety of churches, I cannot help sensing whether these communities of faith are marked by more joy than cynicism, more humility than pride, more truth than pretending, more servanthood than power, more freedom than fear, more generosity than greed, more hope than despair, more grace than condemnation, more love than divisiveness. On his very last night with his disciples, before he faced the cross, Jesus told them that the primary evidence to the world that he came from God would be our unity and love for one another. The churches we build on earth represent the most remarkable of opportunities—to be houses of love and light and hope that point the way to God. Are we filled with a zeal that causes us to pick up our ropes like Jesus in the temple and clean house wherever we can find room for improvement?

As Samantha and I have laid out our challenges for churches of the future to thrive, we recognize that no church at any given time gets an *A* in all areas. We set our hopes high for churches to be built on genuine community and focusing on kids while also making a dramatic difference in meeting real needs in the community. And then there's the gathering on Sundays, working on the gender divide and healing past wounds of exclusion while seeking to build a healthy culture. It's a lot to handle! I believe at any moment most churches are doing well in some areas and are limping in others. But if we realistically assess and define where we are, we can get a little better every week. One step all of us and every church can take is to *love*, because love matters most of all.

Beyond all the strategy, vision, and human effort, what finally makes the church the church is quite basic. Sometimes I have to start by simply writing it down:

- There is a God.
- He has revealed himself in the person of Jesus, who died to be our Savior.
- Life with God is offered through Jesus.
- The most important process going on in the universe is the formation of the human character to become transformed over time toward goodness and love.
- The church is a community of people seeking to follow God together.

Whether your zeal meter is running high and passionately for the church these days or lying low in the basement of apathy, I urge you not to give up on the bride of Christ. I admit there are times the church makes us crazy, and there are times when it becomes our lifeline and greatest joy. Italian religious writer and activist Carlo Carretto captured how back-and-forth we can be about the church in his book *The God Who Comes*:

> How baffling you are, oh Church, and yet how I love you!
>
> How you have made me suffer, and yet how much I owe you!
>
> I should like to see you destroyed, and yet I need your presence.
>
> You have given me so much scandal, and yet you have made me understand sanctity.
>
> I have seen nothing in the world more devoted to obscurity, more compromised, false, and I have touched

nothing more pure, more generous, more beautiful. How often I have wanted to shut the doors of my soul in your face, and how often I have prayed to die in the safety of your arms.

No, I cannot free myself from you, because I am you, although not completely.

And besides, where would I go?

———

I'm feeling tender as I write this morning, looking out over the sparkling waters of the lake in Delavan, a small Wisconsin town just over the Illinois border. This part of my world, including Delavan's sister city, Lake Geneva, is where my love for Jesus and his people has magnified since my high school years. Bill and Dave used to bring our youth group up here for retreats when we would dream together about what a loving community could be, what kind of church might be possible. This is also where I brought my arts team at least twice a year, where we washed one another's feet in the summer, played broom hockey on the ice in the winter, and celebrated moments we got to create together on Sunday mornings. How often we would look at one another and say, "I can't believe *we get to do this!*" Hundreds of small-group leaders from Willow traveled to this area many times for training and community building, and our management team gathered for retreats twice a year in a cottage nearby. Whenever I have needed solitude, this is where I drive, seeking God's presence and guidance and healing. It is my place to get grounded.

I cannot imagine my life without Jesus and his bride, the local church. There have been times when my heart broke over God's people when I thought I might not recover, but I was never willing or even tempted, honestly, to leave. Where else would I go? Jesus transformed my life. Following him and walking with his people has been my pathway to forgiveness, hope, belonging, joy, purpose, and, most of all, love. I am forever grateful for the church, even the broken parts.

I have written from the viewpoint of a church leader but maybe more from the perspective of a mom. Nothing brings me and my husband greater joy these days than seeing our daughters flourish in their own churches. Johanna has a gift for design and a heart that beats for the underresourced in Chicago. She has leveraged who God made her to be by finding people whose home could use a makeover, designing a new space, raising funds to cover costs, and rallying volunteers to make it happen. I love to see her shining eyes when she gets to serve in a role God made her to play as she partners with the local church.

Equally fulfilling for me is seeing Samantha's early days serving at her church on staff. I never pushed either daughter to work for a church. Because I know how stretching and sometimes painful it can be, if anything I nudged them to volunteer without joining a staff. Yet seeing Samantha forming a group of creatives in her Austin church and then joining the teaching team, I know she is right where she belongs. When I hear Samantha teach the Sunday morning message, I can hardly breathe. I am so proud of both my girls, knowing that with all they have seen on the negative side of church, they could easily have bailed, still loving Jesus but not investing in a community of faith. I cannot wait to see the church of tomorrow my grandchildren will help to build!

Samantha and I wrote these words primarily to inspire you to join us as we seek to help create the kind of churches we want to call home. Wherever you find yourself these days, I hope and pray you will elevate your zeal for the church. If all of us choose to be *in*, next Sunday can be beautiful.

SAMANTHA

A funny thing happened while we were writing this book: I became a pastor. Where I had been looking ahead to next Sunday as a congregant, as a friend who wondered if her friends could ever feel home at church, as an artist seeking to bring my gifts to bear in a faith community, as a White woman on my own journey of reckoning and repair, there was now a new dimension to my ministry experience. Now, there was an outlet for all the criticism and dreams I'd pent up in the pews about what church could and shouldn't be. I could help make it! Help shape it! Our small staff of six visionaries (two full-time, the rest of us only a handful of hours a week) would facilitate community, build an engaging kids' ministry, serve the needy in our city, program beautiful services, and heal the gender divide as well as all those the historical church has oppressed and decentered! Ready, break!

Okay, but did you know there is a Sunday *every week*? Every six days there is another one. You finish one, you catch your breath, pick up your head, and it's mother-loving Friday already! After a year of this insanity (fifty-two Sundays!), here is what I would like to say to my snobby self on the other side of the curtain with all her ideas: You know what? People can make their own friends. Service templates are my lifeline. Nonprofits are too slow to respond. And you're welcome that we have *anywhere* for your kids to go!

Unfortunately, I don't think this is how pastors are supposed to sound.

This brings me to another menace lurking in the back of my mind as a newly minted minister: a fear of being found out. Because on top of the relentless schedule and unlimited opportunities to serve more, church leaders work under an unattainable expectation: that they perfectly embody the good news they herald. Oh, if only churches weren't full of us creatures who snooze alarms, forget birthdays, worry over our hair and our health, and, as Annie Dillard writes, "waste most of our energy by spending every waking minute saying hello to ourselves." If only churches weren't so desperately human bound, they could flourish, don't you think?

The good news is, deep down, I don't think anyone wants a perfect church. We want a place where we can learn it's possible to love people *through* what separates us. We want honesty about how hard it is to be in relationship and to do good in the world. We want the people onstage to look a little less put together, be a little less Pollyanna. We want to practice and remember the divine order of death and resurrection. We want to see that love is worth it, even though it's always, *always*, less pretty than we make it sound.

━━

For all the money we gave them, my college had some pretty decrepit theater facilities. One of them, Shanley Pavilion, is a tiny black-box performance space that was built in 1943. It's a legendary place to perform in, and when I was finally cast in a play there, I was thrilled. As we moved in during tech week and began rehearsals, my excitement faded. I was only in a couple of scenes of the two-and-a-half-hour play, so I spent most of my time backstage. While the audience seating area had been cleaned to the extent that college students could clean, no such care had been paid to the dressing rooms or the area behind the set. I remember freezing in a dark, dank, not green, green room staring at the mold in the corner, hugging my feet on the stiff chair in case the rat came to visit, quietly putting on a brave face with the other cast members as we all tried to remember how much we loved doing this.

Back in 1959, sociologist Erving Goffman used the language of *front stage* and *back stage* to describe the way we present ourselves for an audience versus how we behave when no one's watching. Impression management has become a round-the-clock job for all of us, a thankless and exhausting one at that. I tease my mom about how she would have felt being a lead pastor today with the pressure to cultivate and maintain an online presence, to comment on every news story as it unfolds, to churn out snack-sized nuggets of content for an increasingly insatiable audience. She says she would have quit. I don't know about that, but I do think it would have distracted her from the behind-the-scenes work she excels at—maximizing, encouraging, and leading people.

I fear that the pressure church leaders feel to curate an image that is just the right balance of messy and polished, funny and profound, impressive and humble, approachable and austere, to always be ready with an opinion or hot take on whatever the day may bring, has left little time to care for the backstage, which, thanks to social media, is now sort of front stage.

But the real culture of a place is unfiltered, unedited, and un-branded. It is not what we choose for people to see but what they would actually see if they were there all the time. It is the back-stage tour of Shanley Pavilion.

How it feels back there matters not just for staff but for the churchgoers and volunteers too. When we come forward to serve, when we express a concern or ask for support, when we dare to bring forth an idea, when we look to the church to come alongside us for our best days and our worst days, we bump into these in-visible realities. Do our churches spend enough time caring for and maintaining all that takes place backstage? What qualities must I cultivate to contribute to a positive culture in my new role?

I am not used to collaborating over the long haul. Theater people know how to create culture quickly because we have to. A rehearsal process might last six weeks with a two-month run, maybe a short extension if you're lucky. Then the team scatters and moves on to their next projects, with a whole new cast of faces, a new space, and a new audience. So, some customs help leaders form families fast, many of which could be productive in other contexts as well.

Often, directors will establish community agreements early on ("Try ideas before throwing them out," "Speak up if or when you feel unsafe," "Challenge assumptions"), which the team can return to whenever things fall off the rails. Beginnings and endings of meetings are highly intentional. This usually includes daily rituals or check-ins that welcome us into and send us out of our shared time together with care. And there is a great concern for the temporary space *between* each other, which is, after all, where the art is made and exchanged. You will often hear the question "How did that feel for you?" asked of each participant in a rehearsal process. That's probably a question we could ask more of backstage at our churches.

However, as freelancers, we don't stick around long enough to ride out different seasons of life together, to grow and change as people or experience major shifts in our world. Frankly, someone can behave terribly and get hired again and again. We come together for a particular place, time, and purpose. Build a pop-up culture and move on.

Now that I'm in ministry I'm discovering that we're in this to stay. There will (hopefully) be no closing show. It's just this. It's just us. Sunday after Sunday. And we cannot hope to lead anyone where we are not willing to go. To love well over time—to nurture the space between us—will require me to develop some new skills. Namely, I must grow more comfortable with the process of rupture and repair.

———

My friend Carissa is someone you cannot hide from. The first time I met her, I felt her peer deep inside me and knew she was a safe place for my truest self. This is her gift. Her experience as a therapist has given her a front-row seat to the messy movements of the human heart. And she has been in and around church her whole life—as a pastor's kid, attendee, volunteer, staff member, and elder. She now convenes a space for a group of pastors from across the country to process their ministry. From this position she observes how our ministry environments nurture or stifle our transformation.

Growing up, Carissa remembers a church culture where "the hard was hidden." She remembers difficult family issues being addressed in secret because the focus was on "performance, piety, people pleasing, pacifying, and punishment." But she notes a broader cultural shift that has influenced many churches.

"Now, Brené Brown has all of us thinking more about honesty and vulnerability," she said to me. "Which is good. Now we're seeing more of that. But we don't know what to do when it all gets dumped in the middle. It's no use if we're going to revert to our coping mechanisms of fight, flight, freeze, or please. We've got to get past just saying our truth. Now, what do we *do* with it?"

Carissa believes that relational maturity will be a defining characteristic of healthy churches in the years to come. In his book *Emotionally Healthy Spirituality*, Peter Scazzero writes about the stunted emotional health in some of our churches, "The end result of an inability to walk out our beliefs is that our churches and relationships within the church are not qualitatively any different from the world around us." How we wish this weren't so! We long for the culture of a church to be of a different texture from what we experience at school, work, and family gatherings. But we won't be defined by an absence of pain. And we can't stop at vulnerability. Maybe what would be unique is a place where what's hard and what's true lead us *toward* one another, again and again.

Scazzero says this will require maturing out of our narcissism, embracing conflict, checking our assumptions, and establishing mutually agreed-upon expectations. I would add self-awareness to that list. Regarding the church, he writes,

> One of the greatest gifts we can give our world is to be a community of emotionally healthy adults who love well. This will take the power of God and a commitment to learn, grow, and break with unhealthy, destructive patterns that go back generations in our families and cultures—and in some cases, our Christian culture also.

Which, I suppose, brings us back to where we started: People. Community. And the space between us.

In a strange turn of events, Will is more proud than anyone in my family to tell people about my new job. My mom isn't so enthusiastic about me stepping into ministry. She has always championed my dreams wholeheartedly, so her hesitancy is notable. Maybe she had hoped to see me on Broadway. Maybe she worried that my gifts wouldn't be recognized or celebrated. Or maybe she sees the church more clearly than I can yet. She knows that it holds great promise and therefore great capacity to disappoint.

I didn't think *I* wanted to do it either. Ministry wasn't my dream. It was hers. I dreamed of telling stories that pointed to our connection, our responsibility to one another, the possibility of transformation. I was going to tell the stories I learned in church, but I was determined to tell them somewhere else. Somewhere sexier. Somewhere with less baggage and more room for more people. Somewhere I could be proud of.

And yet here I am. Counting down between Sundays.

I can't seem to outrun it.

Maybe because it was where I first felt belonging.

Maybe because watching Will fall in love with what church could be made me want to help make it so.

Maybe because of the Teddy Roosevelt quote that hangs in our hall: "It is not the critic who counts. . . . The credit belongs to the man who is actually in the arena."

Or maybe I'm here because the older I get, the more unwieldy the world reveals itself to be and the fewer answers I have. I have grown up in the age of access, but that hasn't necessarily translated to action.

In her book *Trick Mirror*, Jia Tolentino writes about how my generation's exposure to inequity has left us reeling:

> There was no limit to the amount of misfortune a person could take in via the internet. . . . [A]nd there was no way to calibrate this information correctly—no guidebook for how to expand our hearts to accommodate these simultaneous scales of human experience, no way to teach ourselves to separate the banal from the profound. The internet was dramatically increasing our ability to know about things, while our ability to change things stayed the same, or possibly shrank right in front of us. I had started to feel that the internet would only ever induce this cycle of heartbreak and hardening—a hyper-engagement that would make less sense every day.

Where then can we go to expand our hearts and our ability to change things? Where can we lament the brokenness and celebrate the beauty that the internet slams in front of us with unstoppable speed? Where can we unlearn the *great American lie*—passed down to every generation—that the only proper response is to hoard and protect and control what you can? My friends are disillusioned by a church more preoccupied with belief than with love, but that doesn't mean we don't desperately want to experience God.

Politics is the biggest story that most people I know see themselves as a part of. It's become the dominant, organizing framework—something to sacrifice for, something to connect us all (or at least half of us). I hope my generation stays politically engaged, and Gen Z is already on track to outpace us. Jesus' ministry was undeniably focused on social and economic transformation. But that included the formation of our hearts. I wonder if, as T. S. Eliot says, we dream of "systems so perfect that no one will need to be good." If the political realm was a sufficient school of character formation, it wouldn't produce such cynics.

I believe there are millennials in every city who long for a local expression of love they can participate in. We want to transform our inner *and* outer worlds. We want community that breaks us out of our algorithms and seats us next to those we would never otherwise meet. We want to get offline and experience just how sacred our God-infused world is through what we can touch and taste. We want to learn how to be generous with our time, our talents, and our money (even though in literally every measurable way, we are doing worse financially than our parents. We don't blame you—or maybe we do, but we'll try to let that suitcase go!). We believe in teaching our kids about compassion and freedom, as many of our parents did. We just want those truths to endure. We want them big enough and wide enough to cover not just those at the center but all those who we now see have been excluded. Speaking of which, we *really* want a place where we can unlearn our "isms" and pursue restoration. And we don't want to do it alone.

So, after a decade of choosing a lot of other things, I find myself unexpectedly, or perhaps inevitably, choosing church. Sorry, Mom.

Now, it's chapter seven, and Will and I have spent almost a year in the house we bought in chapter one. We also have a baby on the way. (Books take a long time!) I can't help but wonder what our child's church story will be. If she's a girl . . . if my baby is gay . . . when the questions come . . . when rupture occurs.

It's an old house, as Don warned us. There were a few things we had to get rid of right away: old electrical wiring, a squirrel-sized hole in the siding, and a fire hazard in the attic. Then, there were lots of updates we wanted to make, but, with limited resources, we had to choose what was most urgent. Will couldn't fit under the showerhead, so that moved to the top of the list. The kitchen got a face-lift and Don helped us with our porch, as promised. The windows and roof will have to wait a few years. And then there are other elements—unique features of an older house—that we treasure and wouldn't dream of changing: the hardwood floor and big white shutters.

I see how my mom went through this process when she helped make the church she inherited into a home for her community. And now she (and all my church aunts and uncles) are preparing to hand over the keys. It'll be our turn soon. It's an old house. *You gotta know what you're getting into.* But, as my designer sister would say, "the place has good bones." Someday, my child may look around and have some renovations of their own to suggest—not in an attempt to keep up with some treadmill of relevance or culture or aesthetics but because our collective consciousness continues to evolve, the arc of the universe bending toward justice, as Martin Luther King Jr. prophesied—and so too can our churches.

In her book *Leaving Church*, Barbara Brown Taylor writes,

In a quip that makes the rounds, Jesus preached the coming of the kingdom, but it was the church that came. All these years later, the way many of us are doing church is broken and we know it, even if we do not know what to do about it. We proclaim the priesthood of all believers while we continue with hierarchical clergy, liturgy, and architecture. We follow a Lord who challenged the religious and political institutions of his time while we fund and defend our own. We speak and sing of divine transformation while we do everything in our power to maintain our equilibrium. If redeeming things continue to happen to us in spite of these deep contradictions in our life together, then I think that is because God is faithful even when we are not.

What a relief that the Spirit of God does not depend on us. The river flows, despite us. Perhaps our work is simply to surrender; to notice and cease the activities that have us swimming upstream.

In the quiet of the living room in my new house, I wonder what stories these old walls could tell. Though I've never met them, I think of how intimately connected I am to the families who lived here before us. How we looked out the same window each morning. How we opened the same door to welcome people inside. I wonder if they too loved how the light hit the hallway at dawn.

I try to forgive them when our electrician gives us the quote. (At this point I also consider unchoosing church and choosing electricity as a career instead.) Maybe they didn't know then what we know now about the dangers of aluminum wiring. I extend this same forgiveness on the paint choices. And tiny closets. It's a complex relationship that I have with the ghosts of my house. And the ancestors of my faith.

But I'm grateful they took care of it so that it could become home to me.

We will try to do the same.

Let your continual mercy, O Lord, cleanse and defend your Church;

and, because it cannot continue in safety without your help,

protect and govern it always by your goodness;

through Jesus Christ our Lord,

who lives and reigns with you and the Holy Spirit,

one God, for ever and ever. Amen.

THE BOOK OF COMMON PRAYER

Acknowledgments

We would like to express our gratitude to our agent, Alex Field, for believing in this project from the beginning. We thank our editor, Ethan McCarthy, and the team at InterVarsity Press. Thank you to our early readers—Esha, Carissa, Kelley, Goodie, John, and Nancy—for your invaluable feedback and challenging questions. Thanks to all those who let us share your stories in these pages; for your vulnerability, courage, and trust. And to South Park Church, Willow Creek Community Church, Soul City Church, and Austin New Church . . . thanks for your faithfulness, imperfection, and courage, Sunday after Sunday.

NANCY

Thank you to all the men and women I have had the privilege to coach. Your resilience, innovation, humility, and grace bolster my hope for the future of the church.

God has blessed me with an abundance of friendships—I cannot risk missing any one of your names, but I thank you for your unmistakable role in helping me to feel and know the love of Jesus and keeping me from bailing on the church.

To Johanna—I delight in who you are and still can't believe I get to be your mom. Thank you for your perspective and advocacy for this project. You are my sunshine . . .

Will, I love watching how you love Samantha. Thank you for being my first son.

I dedicated this book to my life partner and husband of forty-one years. Warren, thank you for being the one who walks with me through every season and makes me laugh almost every day. I love you forever.

And to my coauthor, Samantha. You know I am a reluctant writer. This book would not have happened without you stepping up to partner. There wasn't a single moment of this process when I did not burst with gratitude that we got to do this together. I am thrilled that your voice will now be more widely heard. Love you to the moon and back . . .

SAMANTHA

Thank you to my current church family, and the team I get to do ministry with—Jason, Tray, Stephanie, Shea, Lamar, and César. You've restored my hope in Sundays, and beyond.

To Alan Sanders and Laura Schellhardt, for all that you taught me about the craft of writing and the art of noticing.

To my sister, without whom I am not me. And Dad, I could only write about embodied faith because I see you live it. You two should write a book together next; maybe something about the future of flea markets.

Thanks to my husband, against whom my inner critic doesn't stand a chance. It is just as we feared: sharing our lives is making them fly. I love you so.

To the little one who grew inside me as I wrote these words, thanks for the company. Have patience with us: your parents, and your church.

And finally, thanks to my mom. For all you taught me and all the freedom you gave me to evolve. Thank you for surrounding me with stories. You always said if you could line up all the little girls in the world, you'd pick me to be your daughter every time. Well, after thirty-two years, I'd still pick you to be my mom. And collaborator. And friend. I can't believe we got to do this.

About the Authors

Nancy Beach has always been a passionate champion for artists and leaders in the local church. For more than twenty years she served as a teaching pastor and programming director for Willow Creek Community Church in suburban Chicago, building a community of artists who sought to create transformational moments in Sunday morning church services. Currently, Nancy is a leadership coach with the Slingshot Group, helping church leaders and teams to flourish in life and ministry. She is also the author of *An Hour on Sunday* and *Gifted to Lead: The Art of Leading as a Woman in the Church*. Nancy and her husband, Warren, live in the village of Barrington, Illinois, with their dog, Beanie. After forty-one years of marriage, they are happy to say they still choose each other.

Samantha Beach Kiley is a writer and performer working at the intersection of art and faith. Sam serves as the creative arts pastor of Austin New Church and escapes the Texas heat in the summers at Rocky Mountain Repertory Theatre, where she and her husband, Will, both serve as education director. Her plays have been produced in professional and educational settings, as well as in family rooms, children's homes, and hospitals with the national tour of her miniature show, *We the W(h)ee*. Her acting experience includes theater, voiceover, and television, and she is a creative consultant for churches and nonprofits (www.samantha beach.work). Sam and Will live in Austin, Texas, with their daughter, Eloise, and their dog, Rooney.

IVP PRAXIS

EQUIPPING LEADERS FOR MINISTRY

"...TO EQUIP HIS PEOPLE FOR WORKS OF SERVICE,

SO THAT THE BODY OF CHRIST MAY BE BUILT UP."

EPHESIANS 4:12

God has called us to ministry. But it's not enough to have a vision for ministry if you don't have the practical skills for it. Nor is it enough to do the work of ministry if what you do is headed in the wrong direction. We need both vision *and* expertise for effective ministry. We need *praxis*.

Praxis puts theory into practice. It brings cutting-edge ministry expertise from visionary practitioners. You'll find sound biblical and theological foundations for ministry in the real world, with concrete examples for effective action and pastoral ministry. Praxis books are more than the "how to" – they're also the "why to." And because *being* is every bit as important as *doing*, Praxis attends to the inner life of the leader as well as the outer work of ministry. Feed your soul, and feed your ministry.

If you are called to ministry, you know you can't do it on your own. Let Praxis provide the companions you need to equip God's people for life in the kingdom.

www.ivpress.com/praxis